LOST LONDON
IN COLOUR

Browning's Pool, Little Venice, Paddington, *c.* 1908

Off Vauxhall, 1893

A study of the River Thames by an anonymous photographer catches London's river during the frigid winter of 1893. Beached Thames sailing barges are beset by ice, and old Lambeth Bridge (1862) looms through the freezing mist (see also page 21).

LOST LONDON
IN COLOUR

BRIAN GIRLING

AMBERLEY

Nile Street Shops, Hoxton (Shoreditch), c. 1906

First published 2013

Amberley Publishing
The Hill, Stroud, Gloucestershire, GL5 4EP
www.amberley-books.com

Copyright © Brian Girling, 2013

The right of Brian Girling to be identified as the
Author of this work has been asserted in accordance with
the Copyrights, Designs and Patents Act 1988.

ISBN 978 1 4456 1502 8 (print)
ISBN 978 1 4456 1512 7 (ebook)

British Library Cataloguing in Publication Data.
A catalogue record for this book is available from the
British Library.

Typesetting by Amberley Publishing.
Printed in Great Britain.

Seven Dials, Holborn, c. 1880

Located between multicultural Soho, poverty stricken St Giles and the market area of Covent Garden, Seven Dials was a lively neighbourhood of Victorian London. It originated in the 1690s on marshy St Giles Field with a layout of narrow streets radiating out from a small circus more typical of Paris than London. As seen in this tinted glass-lantern slide, life here typified that of many ordinary neighbourhoods in Victorian times, with bustling streets and narrow overcrowded tenements above basic domestic shops and the ever present corner pub. Seven Dials remained too poor to afford much rebuilding, but it would survive the Blitz and the later twentieth century would see the fortunes of the scruffy old district revive with gentrification spreading outwards from Covent Garden following the departure of the fruit and vegetable merchants from the market and its warehouses. The essential character of Seven Dials would remain and new money would attract smart shops, while the little circus would see the return (in replica) of a column sundial put up in 1694 but removed in 1773. Queen Beatrix of the Netherlands would unveil the revived column on 29 June 1989. (*Photograph by courtesy of Gareth Long*)

Oxford Street by Orchard Street, *c.* 1895

Pictured by an amateur photographer, this was London's premier shopping street before the arrival of its grandest department stores. Small shops on the left would provide a site for Marks & Spencer's flagship store (1932), while beyond Orchard Street the future site of the mighty Selfridge's (1909) was made up of a lengthy terrace of far more modest shops (see also pages 35, 36 and 51).

INTRODUCTION

London has always provided an inspirational spectacle for the artist and photographer, and when the ethereal beauty of London's earliest known photograph (of Charing Cross) was created by the daguerreotype process in 1839, it was the first step towards an eventual treasury of London photographs which would document the changing face of the capital and its inhabitants through the decades. The 1850s brought refinements to photographic processes and with them came new mediums for conveying the image, including cabinet cards, the *carte-de-visite* and the stereoscopic card, which gave a 3D effect when viewed through a stereoscope, a popular source of home entertainment in Victorian times. Glass-lantern slides for projection gave perhaps the most stunningly detailed images from square or circular images, especially when hand tinting added realism to the monochrome originals. While hand colouring to all types of photographs added to what was already a costly indulgence, it was a phenomenon that arrived from the Continent in the 1890s and was popularised in the 1900s, which brought affordable coloured images within reach of everyone – it was the picture postcard.

The year 1894 saw the first British picture postcard, but for the remainder of the century the Post Office applied drastic restrictions on the size of the card and how it could be presented: the message and the picture had to be fitted into a tiny space on one side, leaving the whole of the other side for the address. Even so, the halfpenny postage rate alone ensured the picture postcard's popularity. Early postcard images tended to be artist derived. However, with the 1900s and an easing of Post Office regulations the whole of one side could be devoted to the picture. This brought about the introduction of a new type of postcard: the 'real photograph', which was an actual photograph with a printed back for the message and stamp.

By 1903, teams of postcard photographers set about recording this country as never before, not only in popular areas for the tourist trade, like central London, but also in local neighbourhoods, sometimes with such intensity that in some localities every street appeared on at least one card. This great flood of new cheap pictures triggered a collecting craze, which soon outstripped that of the *carte-de-visite* some fifty years earlier, and there were few households that did not have a postcard album. In an era of monochrome photography, there was still plentiful employment for hand colourists although new techniques in colour printing were evolving, giving new realism to some postcards from the Edwardian age. The Photochrom Company of Tunbridge Wells was particularly successful with its 'Celesque' and other series of fine colour cards, as were J. Salmon Ltd of Sevenoaks and the fine art publishers Raphael Tuck & Sons who introduced the Oilette. This was a colourful and popular range of postcards within which were many whose origin was a monochrome photograph but retouched in colour to resemble a painting, albeit a rather idealised one.

The illustrations for this book are principally sourced from the vast postcard output of the first four decades of the twentieth century, supplemented by *cartes-de-visite*, stereoscopic cards and glass-lantern slides. There are also some colour-enhanced images from Victorian photograph albums and a small selection from a colour snapshot album of the 1960s alongside colour images from the 1940s.

The following pages document some of the changes in appearance and style of a great world city whose haphazard growth had created fascinating contrasts of wealth and poverty, often in adjoining streets. A small selection of images from the late 1850s and early 1860s picture a city that was essentially Georgian in character and still lacking some of the famed and familiar landmarks which would come to symbolise London, including Tower Bridge, Westminster Cathedral, Admiralty Arch and the Thames embankments. The iconic Underground was still a vision for the future and Piccadilly Circus remained an unremarkable crossroads along a still youthful Regent Street. Other new 'sights' included the rebuilt Palace of Westminster, but ancient Westminster Abbey and St Paul's Cathedral endured amid surroundings that would be barely recognisable today. Later photographs show London in its Victorian prosperity with the Thames crowded by the maritime trade, teeming streets and the vast choice of shopping options that only a great city can provide. Edwardian and later postcards chart the rise of the cinema in London alongside an already rich theatrical tradition, while a further sequence explores a city where something always seemed to be happening, either *en fête* with decorated streets for a royal event or hosting a spectacular national exhibition.

There is also a look at London's historic transport system with its horse buses, trams and the primitive contraptions that were London's first motorbuses and taxicabs.

A concluding sequence explores something of Londoners' own London: the old villages and suburbs that were caught up in the capital's great expansions, many of them now 'inner London'.

Through looking at old photographs we may have become accustomed to regarding the London of our ancestors as a place of sepia and grey monochrome, but of course it was not – it is hoped the following pages will dispel that illusion.

ACKNOWLEDGEMENTS

I would like to thank everyone who has helped with the production of this book, particularly those who have made pictorial contributions, including Judge's Postcards of Hastings, The Imperial War Museum, Gareth Long and the host of unknown photographers whose names do not always grace their work. Additional research by Ian Vanlint is also gratefully acknowledged.

A SELECT BIBLIOGRAPHY

Burstein, Diane, *London Then and Now*
Eyles, Alan and Skone, Keith, *London's West End Cinemas*
Hobhouse, Hermione, *Lost London*
Jackson, Peter, *Walks in Old London*
Leboff, David, *London's Underground Stations*
Pevsner, Nikolaus, *The Buildings of England: London Vols 1–6*
Stamp, Gavin, *The Changing Metropolis*
Weinreb, Ben and Hibbert, Christopher, *The London Encyclopaedia*

The Upper Pool of London from London Bridge, *c.* 1880

London exists because of its river, the Thames, and the reach of it, the place where it all began nearly 2,000 years ago, is pictured on this Victorian lantern slide. This was the time when occupying Romans set up Londinium, a small trading port, and bridged the wide sluggish river they called Tamesis. The site of a series of Roman bridges and the famous medieval one that succeeded them in 1176 runs through the foreground of the picture, which was photographed when the Port of London was at the height of its Victorian prosperity. Then, such was the press of shipping awaiting use of the docking facilities, many vessels were obliged to moor far out into the tideway, including, as seen here, an 'ice-ship', the property of George Stevenson, ice merchant and fishmonger. Stevenson traded from premises in Lower Thames Street by Billingsgate, London's ancient wholesale fish market.

The photographer's viewpoint was London Bridge, the new crossing built in 1831 slightly upstream of the medieval bridge, but as seen here, an important part of the modern view is missing – it would be another decade before the most iconic of London landmarks that is Tower Bridge would begin to grace the river.

The latter part of the twentieth century would see the riverside here transformed following the relocation far downstream of the docks and fish market and the arrival of modern office blocks, with a Thames walkway opening up the river for all to enjoy.

London Bridge from Borough High Street, Southwark, *c.* 1881

Opened by King William IV and Queen Adelaide on 1 August 1831, Rennie's London Bridge was a mere fifty years old when photographed for this lantern slide, but London's busiest bridge was already clogged by an all too familiar traffic jam. The mass of omnibuses, cabs and wagons fought their way into and out of the City of London on the opposite bank with heavy dockland traffic and wagons from nearby Borough Market adding to the mêlée. Close by, London Bridge station had opened in 1836, and as passenger numbers grew in the great Victorian railway expansion, the daily ritual of arrival and departure of city workers added to the bridge's workload. The bridge was widened in 1902–04 and replaced entirely in 1972, but many mourned the lost elegance of Rennie's design, which modern concrete failed to replicate. To the right of the view Fennings Wharf's impressive warehouse was one of a long line of such structures along the river's south bank, while over the Thames and into the city the hall of the Worshipful Company of Fishmongers (1834) is seen centre left. To the right the tower of the church of St Magnus-the-Martyr (begun 1668) marks the point where old London Bridge once crossed the river.

London Bridge, *c.* 1930

A colourful postcard by J. Salmon Ltd pictures Rennie's bridge against a backdrop of city wharves and the recently completed Adelaide House, as yet not blackened by London's smoky air.

8175. LONDON BRIDGE.

St Paul's Cathedral and Queenhithe from Southwark Bridge, *c.* 1858
This image from one half of a stereoscopic card offers a rare glimpse of part of the old city waterfront before a wave of warehouse building in the later Victorian era began to transform it. This was London's original Docklands and the inlet of Queenhithe, which was known to the Saxons as Aetheredeshyth, was one of its more important harbours. As seen here, there are still remnants of the houses put up after the Great Fire of 1666 and a large tree still shades Queenhithe's dock and the neighbouring King's Arms pub. The warehouse building would soon change the scene but for the moment Bull Wharf and White Kennet Wharf, with their ramshackle facilities, linger on.

Tower Bridge, *c.* 1895
London had to wait for more than a millennium before another bridge was built on the seaward side of London Bridge, but when one arose in 1894 it did so in the grandest style with this mighty Gothic gateway to the oldest part of the Port of London. The bridge, beloved of Londoners and visitors alike, allied spectacular architecture with Victorian inventiveness, the hydraulically operated bascules being lifted to allow the passage of larger ships upstream. This lantern slide captures its earliest days.

Puddle Dock, Blackfriars, *c.* 1920 (Left) and *c.* 1968 (Below)

In medieval times, this was a place where horses were brought to water and later, with commercialism and wharfage spreading along the river, a refuge for barges from the river's tidal currents. The sheer wall on the left of the older picture was once part of City Mills (1850), a lofty building which was used a various times for milling, tin plating and latterly for warehousing before the Blitz reduced it to a shell. It would achieve more lasting fame in 1959 when what remained of it would be reborn as the Mermaid Theatre, Lord Miles' visionary project to bring live theatre back to the City of London. At first, the Mermaid would enjoy its riverside location, but in the 1960s old Puddle Dock would be in-filled and more land reclaimed from the river for the creation of the Blackfriars Underpass and its associated roads (below). This would divorce the Mermaid from the Thames and give Puddle Dock a new role as a busy highway. The snapshot from the 1960s shows building work in progress.

Bankside Power Station from the City of London, 1960s
An amateur photographer's snapshot gives a reminder of the dereliction that prevailed along the city waterfront for some decades following the Second World War. Old maritime Upper Thames Street was marked by bombsites and crumbling warehouses, but in time, bright new buildings would arise, including new riverside premises for the City of London School for Boys (1983–86), but the concrete brutalism seen towards Blackfriars has little visual appeal. Across the river, Bankside Power Station, built in 1963 to the designs of Sir Giles Gilbert Scott, was a new facility but a short lived one – it closed in 1980 only to reopen in 2002 as Tate Modern, the national museum of modern art.

The Thames from the Monument to the Great Fire of London, 1960s
The third in this sequence of snapshots finds their photographer at the top of this famed viewpoint looking out over a mainly low-rise capital and a working river where barges are moored off a wharf-lined Bermondsey shore at Pickle Herring Street, the future site of City Hall (2002), headquarters of the Greater London Authority. A smoke-blackened Tower Bridge awaits its future clean-up and the trees to its left mark the precincts of the Tower of London, the great fortress begun by William the Conqueror in 1077. In the foreground is Custom House, as rebuilt in 1817, and Billingsgate Market, whose activities moved downstream in 1982. Also seen is a partly demolished Coal Exchange, a road-widening casualty.

LONDON DOCKS ENTRANCE, LEMAN STREET.

London Docks, *c.* 1906

For centuries, the City of London together with the Southwark and Bermondsey riverfronts were London's Docklands, but as the port's maritime trade developed further, new facilities in the form of enclosed docks were built further downstream to handle larger ships and cargoes. West India Docks opened at the Isle of Dogs in 1802, while closer to the city, London Docks at Wapping commenced its activities in 1805 – cargoes of tobacco with wine and spirits were handled here. In a pair of postcards by local publisher Charles Fielding, the upper one shows the landward entrance to the docks from Nightingale Lane (now Thomas More Street), while the lower one was photographed from the world's first cast-iron swing bridge, which carried Wapping High Street's carriageway over the dock entrance from the river. Frequent openings of the bridge to let the ships through caused traffic chaos in this industrious quarter.

Pier Head, Wapping, *c.* 1906

Shipping from the Thames passed through this narrow entrance and into Wapping Basin from where it could access the larger Western Dock in the London Dock complex. The docks would close in 1969 with a leafy garden replacing the waterway, and regeneration creating a fashionable residential area out of preserved warehouses and the former dock official's houses seen here. This is a dramatic contrast to earlier centuries when, fuelled by an astonishing number of taverns and beer houses, Wapping was a rip-roaring 'sailor town' with a notorious reputation.

Tunnel Pier, Wapping, *c.* 1906

This facility was provided by the Port of London Authority to handle passenger traffic on the river, which then included London County Council's service of steam boats. These 'penny steamers' did not attract enough business to remain viable and the service finished in 1907. Tunnel Pier was named after the first tunnel in the world to pass under a major river and was constructed from 1825 to 1843 to plans by Brunel. Opening as a pedestrian route, it was later adapted to take the steam trains of the East London Railway linking Wapping with Rotherhithe. These are more views by the local postcard man, Charles Fielding.

Blackwall Pier and Steamer Braemar Castle entering East India Dock.

Blackwall Pier, Poplar, *c*. 1906

An important passenger terminal on the river, Blackwall's facilities allowed travellers to journey from Fenchurch Street station via the London & Blackwall Railway and transfer to one of the ships which served Continental and British ports. Blackwall's station closed in 1926 and today this historic area, once noted for its shipbuilding industry, is overlooked by the skyscrapers of modern Docklands at Canary Wharf. The postcard is by Stengel & Co., whose series of views covered much of Europe during the Edwardian era.

Surrey Commercial Docks, *c*. 1908

The southern bank of the Thames is an equally historic Dockland area, with Surrey Commercial Docks part of a vast system of enclosed wet docks created on a marshy Thames peninsular between the old naval and shipbuilding centre of Deptford to the east and the riverside village of Rotherhithe to the west. Howland Great Wet Dock was working as early as 1697 – it was later renamed Greenland Dock and specialised in cargoes of timber. The Surreys closed in 1970 and a period of dereliction preceded a rebirth as a series of new residential neighbourhoods, with Greenland Dock retaining its waters for a variety of aquatic leisure pursuits.

A view of Surrey Commercial Docks, London, S. E.

**The Southwark Riverfront from the Tower of London,
c. 1905**
With its rows of warehouses and wharves, the river's
south bank lacked the photogenic appeal of its northern
counterpart and most postcard publishers tended to
ignore it. This example by a French publisher is therefore
something of a rarity but it nicely pictures the working
river in Edwardian times. In the far distance, the outlines
of London Bridge and Southwark Cathedral, which date
from the thirteenth century, may be seen.

Old Waterloo Bridge and Somerset House, c. 1905
Some of the finest views of the grandest reach of the Thames are
famously had from Waterloo Bridge, and the first incarnation of
it came in 1817 when it added a new crossing between existing
Blackfriars and Westminster Bridges. Subsidence hastened the
demise of the old bridge in 1936 but its modern replacement
(1937–42) is a wonderfully graceful affair. The long terrace of
Somerset House is seen beyond the bridge and is older, having
been built in 1776 on the site of a sixteenth-century palace.

The Thames Embankment, London.

The Victoria Embankment from Hungerford Bridge, *c.* 1904 – Day to Night Transformation Postcard

The Victorians and Edwardians were adept at altering and adapting original monochrome photographs to create a variety of special effects. Stereoscopic pictures were popular as were day to night transformation scenes where the effect varied from day, through twilight to night depending on the viewing conditions. This style of 'transparency' was used for Continental postcards in the 1890s, and as postcards gained in popularity in Britain during the 1900s the style caught on here too. This one by the German publisher Hartmann is a typical example, the effect made possible by layers of transparent paper behind a chromolithographed front for the 'daytime' scene. As may be seen, however, a written message could disrupt the 'night' scene.

The view, which has distant origins as a photograph, portrays the beginning of the river's great curve towards Blackfriars, with distant Waterloo Bridge and the prominent Hotels Cecil (1885) and Savoy (1889) with Charing Cross Pier in the foreground.

River Fog, Tower Bridge from the Wapping Shore, *c.* 1910
Photographer and postcard publisher Fred Judge of Hastings was a skilful portrayer of the moods and atmosphere of early twentieth-century London and its river, and his lengthy series of London postcards includes many beautiful and innovative images. The cards are usually presented in a rich sepia finish but here colour has added a new dimension. The photographs were created at a time when London had a well deserved reputation as a foggy city – the river's mists were frequently thickened by the vapours from countless domestic coal fires, factories and steam locomotives, and the setting sun would often be lost in a brownish haze.

By Westminster Bridge, *c.* 1910
Boadicea in her chariot surveys a murky scene as a tram turns towards Westminster Bridge and south London. (*Courtesy of Judges Postcards, Hastings*)

The Victoria Embankment from Westminster Bridge, *c.* **1880**

This reach of the Thames has always made an impressive spectacle even in much earlier times when houses, private gardens and assorted lowly buildings connected with life on the river came down to the water's edge. The majestic riverscape we know today began to take shape from 1862 to 1870 with the construction of Victoria Embankment, which cleverly combines a much-needed sewerage system, an underground railway and a grand tree-lined Thames Boulevard, all on 37 acres of land reclaimed from the river. The scheme was masterminded by the Metropolitan Board of Works' chief engineer, Sir Joseph Bazalgette, whose other work included Albert and Chelsea Embankments. In this early view, notable landmarks – New Scotland Yard (1890); Whitehall Court, built in the French Renaissance style in 1884; and the Hotel Metropole (1885) – have yet to arrive, while the youthful saplings are still a modest feature. Further along, the cavernous train shed of Charing Cross station rises up – it was built on the site of Hungerford Market (1682–1860). The photographer of this lantern slide has preserved one of those sparkling London days when the smoke has blown away and all is gleaming bright in the sunshine – the passengers on the paddle steamer by Westminster Pier would have enjoyed their river trip on such a day.

The Palace of Westminster (the Houses of Parliament) from Lambeth, 1893
This masterpiece of the Gothic Revival style resulted from the rebuilding of the Palace of Westminster by Charles Barry following the destruction of the old palace by fire in 1834. Barry's creation has an awesome beauty when seen from most angles, but when its towers, pinnacles and spires are blurred by the river's mists there is a magical quality to the river here, one which photographers and artists, including Monet and Turner, have been inspired to preserve. The palace is seen here through the freezing mist of 1893's bitter winter as ice coats the staging by the Lambeth shore.

The Frozen Thames at Vauxhall, 1893
The Thames was once broader and shallower, with tides that flowed with less vigour than in the present day. The river could then freeze more easily but now ice is only seen during the most severe winters, as in these images from a Victorian photographer's album. Here the sailing barges are stranded on an icy shore and old Lambeth Bridge is almost lost in the freezing mist.

Westminster Bridge Road, Lambeth, 1897

The first Westminster Bridge opened in 1750 and was served by the 'New Road' that was built for it. The old bridge was replaced in 1862 by a new crossing in cast iron with Charles Barry as architectural consultant. The New Road became Westminster Bridge Road, which is seen here at a time of national rejoicing as Queen Victoria celebrates her Diamond Jubilee on 22 June 1897 – a grand royal procession passed this way following a Service of Thanksgiving at St Paul's Cathedral. The buildings on the right mark the future site of County Hall, the headquarters of London County Council – this would open in stages from 1922.

Old Hungerford Bridge, *c.* 1858

Isambard Kingdom Brunel's elegant pedestrian bridge crossed the Thames at its widest point in central London, but its life would be brief. It opened in 1845 but it would be sacrificed by 1860 for a railway bridge to serve the new Charing Cross station, although parts of the structure would be re-used for Brunel's Clifton Suspension Bridge. This stereo card shows some of the moorings and lowly property about to be swept away for the new Victoria Embankment.

Millbank Street, Abingdon Street and Victoria Tower, Palace of Westminster, *c.* 1867

The sight of Charles Barry's 323-foot tower, which was finished in 1860, would have been astonishing for the Victorian Londoners who inhabited this now lost riverside community of Georgian terraces, local shops, wharves and ramshackle workshops that bordered the Palace of Westminster. Demolition and road widening through the decades would eventually lead to the more open aspect to the parliamentary precinct we know today, with the Victoria Tower Gardens providing its opulent greenery from 1911. The image comes from a stereoscopic card and reveals the Portman Arms pub on the Wood Street (now Great Peter Street) corner.

Westminster Abbey from Victoria Street, *c.* 1865

The first Westminster Abbey is believed to have been built in the eighth century on Thorney Island, a modest eminence amid the Thames marshland. The Abbey we know today occupies the same site and is a glorious mixture of styles from the millennium, which has shaped its growth – the prominent west towers were added in 1745. In this stereo view by Valentine Blanchard, the Abbey is seen from Victoria Street, a new road in a series of ambitious projects designed to improve communications in the capital. This one cut through a rough quarter of dilapidated slums in the 1860s but empty building sites remained along it for many years afterwards. The backs of old houses in Dean Street (now Great Smith Street) highlight Victoria Street's unfinished look. Westminster Palace Hotel (1861) is on the left.

The Royal Aquarium and Westminster Hospital, Storey's Gate, *c.* 1895

While Westminster Abbey endures through the centuries its surroundings change, as illustrated by this view from a Victorian photographer's album. These now lost buildings include the Royal Aquarium, centre, a palm-filled place of public entertainment built in 1876 and featuring fish tanks, a skating rink and a theatre for music hall performances. Success was elusive, however, and from 1905–11 the Methodist church's central hall would take the site. Westminster Hospital opened in 1834 but would move to new premises in Horseferry Road in 1939. The Queen Elizabeth II Conference Centre is here now.

Strand by Villiers Street, *c.* 1885
The street had its origins in Roman times and was named through its proximity to the river and its foreshore or 'strand'. Land reclamation pushed the river away through the centuries but the steeply graded streets off to the right of the view hint at the ancient landscape; the slopes were the riverbank and an old watergate can still be seen at the foot of Buckingham Street. This lantern slide shows the populous, shop-lined street of Victorian times.

Charing Cross Station and Strand, *c.* 1918
The South Eastern Railway's station opened on 11 January 1864 and the hotel above it on 15 May 1865, complete with a replica Eleanor Cross in the station's forecourt. This recreated one of the original crosses set up to mark the resting places of the funeral cortège of Queen Eleanor, wife of Edward I – the Queen was interred in Westminster Abbey in 1290. The postcard by J. Salmon in their 'Vindictive' series illustrates the colourful and detailed printing style that emerged in the 1910s. The traffic is entirely motorised here.

Trafalgar Square, c. 1868

Admiral Nelson's famous victory at the Battle of Trafalgar in 1805 is commemorated with this grand and much-loved public space that gradually took shape from the 1830s – the granite column topped by a statue of Nelson was finished in 1844. This vintage stereo card pictures the square's southern side and includes Northumberland House, a grandiose Jacobean mansion that was demolished to allow the creation of a new street, Northumberland Avenue. This opened in 1876 as a new route to the still youthful Victoria Embankment. Trafalgar Square is known for its fountains – modest Victorian ones seen here dated from 1845 with more sprightly replacements appearing in 1939. The mermaids and mermen that contribute to the water-play are products of the post-war years.

Trafalgar Square from Spring Gardens, c. 1858

The square is seen from the south-west and shows St Martin-in-the-Fields, Morley's Hotel (the site of South Africa House), and the Strand with Northumberland House at the far right. Nelson is seen on his column, as yet unguarded by Landseer's quartet of lions – they would take up their duties in 1867. A sign on the lamppost points the way to St Matthew's Episcopal chapel (1731) in Spring Gardens – its site would be taken as part of the Admiralty Arch construction from 1911.

Cockspur Street, *c.* 1885

This is one of the places in Westminster whose name is thought to have derived from the ancient 'sport' of cockfighting – the birds had their spurs fitted here before they were taken to the cockpits around St James's Park. The Regency buildings seen here are a product of the 1820s, a time when John Nash's remodelling of parts of the West End introduced the new Regent Street and included improvements to Pall Mall and Haymarket. The building to the left is from that period and contained the Pall Mall Restaurant where in 1871 the Rugby Football Union was founded – a plaque on the wall of the present building, Oceanic House (1906), records the event. Beyond the row of shops and into Trafalgar Square is a surprisingly little changed scene with the Grand Hotel (1881) on the Northumberland Avenue corner, and, as ever, Nelson on his column. This lantern slide reveals some early traffic control with a 'keep left' sign in the foreground.

The Carlton Hotel from Cockspur Street, *c.* 1908

This fine building opened in 1899 but would be tragically demolished in 1957 for a visually destructive tower block. The Regency houses to the right would also go but the equestrian statue of King George III remains in place. This Oilette postcard, a photograph retouched to resemble a painting, records some needlessly lost elegance in the old West End.

Crossing the Square, Trafalgar Square from Charing Cross, *c.* 1890
An amateur's lantern slide captures a moment as an elegantly clothed couple dodge the horse-drawn traffic. Their background is the equestrian statue of King Charles I (1633), Britain's oldest bronze statue. The southern side of Trafalgar Square is part of Charing Cross, so named from the Eleanor Cross, which stood on the statue site from around 1293.

Trafalgar Square and Environs, *c.* 1920
With the rise of aviation in the 1900s and 1910s, aerial view postcards like this became popular with those who were intrigued by seeing their localities from this novel perspective. While most of the early cards were in monochrome, this one was unusual with its colour tinting. Famous landmarks abound in this part of London and among those on view here are The Mall, which was laid out in 1662, and its grand entry point, Admiralty Arch, which dates from 1911. Above it is Trafalgar Square with the National Gallery (1838) and the gleaming steeple of St Martin-in-the-Fields (1726) standing out well. Leicester Square and Soho are off to the left, while Covent Garden and its fruit and vegetable market are at the top right.

LONDON. VIEW FROM THE AIR ABOVE ADMIRALTY ARCH.

Piccadilly Circus from Coventry Street, *c.* 1905

Piccadilly Circus is known worldwide as the electric heart of London's West End but its origins were far more sober. It began at the point where Nash's grand new thoroughfare Regent Street crossed an existing street, Piccadilly, creating a new crossroads called Regent Circus South. The buildings were a circle of matching quadrants in the still-familiar style of Oxford Circus, the old Regent Circus North. The tiny scale of the circus changed in 1886 when another new road, Shaftesbury Avenue, and its associated property clearances created the larger space so familiar today. The Shaftesbury Memorial Fountain 'Eros' arrived in 1893. This German printed postcard catches one of Nash's surviving quadrants, left, with Swan & Edgar's store linking Piccadilly with the graceful curve of Regent Street.

Piccadilly Circus by Regent Street, 1890s

There is little in this amateur photographer's study to hint at the transformation that would soon see Piccadilly Circus evolve into a global meeting point and a focus for London's nightlife. Swan & Edgar's store, left, and the County Fire Office, right, would be rebuilt in 1924 in the grander style of a redesigned Regent Street.

Piccadilly Circus, *c.* 1949

The 1940s was London's darkest decade with wartime blackouts and post-war austerity dimming Piccadilly's famous lights and much else besides. In this scene from a Viewmaster stereo transparency life is returning to near normality and there is a bright new bus to contrast with the war-battered examples seen towards Shaftesbury Avenue. Huge crowds gathered here on 3 April 1949 to witness the 'Great Switch On' of the Piccadilly lights after the blackout years.

Regent Street Looking Towards Piccadilly Circus, *c.* 1918

This postcard in J. Salmon's 'Guildhall' series illustrates the beginning of the street's transition from Nash's clean-cut designs of the 1810s to the monumental scale of the street's rebuilding a century later, with Norman Shaw's Piccadilly Hotel representing the new order. Nash's gracefully curving buildings to the left included the Café-Royal (1865), an opulent café-restaurant that was regularly patronised by artists and writers, including Oscar Wilde, Aubrey Beardsley and Augustus John.

Piccadilly and Burlington House, *c.* 1880

Piccadilly is an old road to the west, built up from the seventeenth century and always a fashionable address. Burlington House, left, was just one of the grand mansions of the nobility that could be found along its length and although parts of it are much altered, it remains the last of its kind here. Burlington House is home to the Royal Academy of Arts (founded 1768) while other learned societies are also based here. This glass-lantern slide depicts the Victorian buildings along the Piccadilly frontage, the carriage and cab-filled street leading towards the far distance where Piccadilly Circus as we know it had yet to arrive – the building line is seen running through the old circular crossroads and into Coventry Street.

Piccadilly Looking West, *c.* 1920

This Salmon postcard shows how Piccadilly was widened in the early twentieth century, with the Piccadilly Hotel (1908) on the right on the new building line with older properties by Swallow Street representing the narrower thoroughfare of old.

Piccadilly by Down Street, 1897

It is 1897 and the grand stone-fronted town houses that look out over Green Park are bedecked with flags and bunting for Queen Victoria's Diamond Jubilee. The Queen's jubilee parade would pass this way and there are viewing stands for the privileged few in this aristocratic quarter of Mayfair.

Horse Guards Parade from St James's Park, *c*. 1858

An early stereo card pictures the Horse Guards Building (1745) overlooking the celebrated parade ground where great military and royal displays, including Trooping the Colour, continue to be enacted. The area of Horse Guards Parade was formerly the tilt yard of Whitehall Palace, which was largely burnt down in 1698. The purist may disapprove of this photographer's composition, but in the world of the stereoscopic image it was desirable to include a prominent element in the foreground to accentuate the stereo effect when seen through a viewer. Here it is one of the park's pre-Victorian street lamps, its lantern topped by a crown and its column featuring the royal cipher G IVR, showing that it first illuminated the way during the reign of George IV (1820–30). Several of these historic lamps remain in use in the park.

282. King Frost in St. James' Park.

Winter in St James's Park, *c.* 1906

Created in the reign of Henry VIII as a royal hunting reserve, St James's is the oldest of central London's Royal Parks, having opened to the public in the reign of Charles II. The park is distinguished by its lake, which had been formed when several ponds were united as a straight canal before the present irregular shape was created in the 1820s. The lake with its islands attracts abundant wildfowl, which is seen here braving an icy Edwardian winter.

St James's Park from Duke of York Steps, Waterloo Place, *c.* 1908

The memorial to the Duke of York was erected from 1831–34, since which time its 137-foot column and statue has made a prominent landmark in the West End. Taking advantage of the natural slope of the land, Duke of York Steps lead down to The Mall and there is a fine view of the great ceremonial square of Horse Guards Parade. This Oilette postcard includes some autumn tints.

Hyde Park Corner, London.

Hyde Park Corner, *c.* 1918

Once styled the busiest corner in the world, the place where Hyde Park, Knightsbridge, Belgravia and Mayfair meet has long been notorious for its traffic, although the opening of an underpass in modern times eased the flow. In the 1820s, there were plans to create a grand western entrance to London and part of what was conceived can still be seen, in the shape of the screen designed by Decimus Burton at the entrance to Hyde Park. St George's Hospital (1833) is seen on the left; the building would become the Lanesborough Hotel following the hospital's removal to Tooting in 1980. The public space looks rather empty in this view compared with the modern layout, which includes military memorials and lawns to link two Royal Parks. The postcard is by H. C. Bromide Co. and was printed in Prussia.

Park Lane by Hertford Street, *c.* 1908

In its nineteenth century heyday, there were grand mansions and bow-fronted town houses overlooking Hyde Park, and while a little of this remains, much rebuilding during the interwar years and conversion of the carriageways to high-speed motor routes has cost Mayfair's grand promenade much of its aristocratic atmosphere. As ever, this Oilette postcard gives an idealised vision with the towering London Hilton Hotel an as yet unimagined intrusion to come.

LONDON. PARK LANE.

130   LONDON W. – The Marble Arch E. – LL.

Marble Arch, *c.* 1906

Marble Arch was another creation of the prolific John Nash, and when finished in 1833 the arch formed a ceremonial entrance to the forecourt of Buckingham Palace. Removal in 1851 took the arch close to a site beside what was until the eighteenth century the notorious Tyburn Gallows. As seen in this postcard by French publisher Louis Levy, Marble Arch made a fine entrance to Hyde Park, but increasing road traffic and a variety of road layouts would soon divorce the arch from the park.

The view looks towards the shopper's paradise of Oxford Street, effectively London's 'High Street', while to the left the town houses by Edgware Road would give way in 1928 to the grandiose Regal (later Odeon) cinema.

LONDON: OXFORD STREET.

Oxford Street by Gilbert Street, *c.* 1919

The capital's premier shopping street had its origins as a Roman road to the west and throughout many centuries it remained a rural highway. When organised building began from the late seventeenth century through to the early nineteenth century, residential properties predominated, but when the stylish new Regent Street crossed the old road from the late 1810s, some of the terraced houses acquired shopfronts with the famous department stores beginning to appear in the 1860s. With the twentieth century came Selfridge's, the spectacular store founded by American entrepreneur Gordon Selfridge in 1909. This Salmon view pictures the half-completed frontage, which would not be finished until 1927, and beside it some of the small properties, which once typified old Oxford Street.

Oxford Street by Holles Street, 1943

It is wartime and one of Oxford Street's enduring businesses, John Lewis, has been laid low by fire following an air raid in 1940. The site, however, has been put to good use with a series of government-held exhibitions of wartime industry – the Army Exhibition is in progress in this colour photograph. In the background is D. H. Evans, another of Oxford Street's retailing giants – it looks unscathed here. The John Lewis store would rise again from 1958. (*Photograph by courtesy of the Imperial War Museum, London, Ref. TR1143*)

Oxford Circus and Regent Street, c. 1906

Laid out as Regent Circus North, this crossroads was part of Nash's groundbreaking Regent Street, but unlike its southern counterpart, Piccadilly Circus, the northern circus has retained its original dimensions despite the rebuilding of the 1920s. The Edwardian postcard by Louis Levy pictures the original Nash buildings – that to the right housing an early incarnation of another great store, Peter Robinson, which sprung from a modest linen-draper's shop set up in 1833.

138 LONDON W. — Oxford Circus N. — LL.

Cavendish Square, the South Side by Holles Street, *c.* 1906

Grand garden squares have long provided homes for London's aristocracy and many indeed are the houses adorned with 'blue plaques' telling of the notable people who have resided within. Cavendish Square, just behind Oxford Street, has a place among the grandest of them and can boast many noteworthy past residents including Horatio Nelson and his wife; Prime Minister Herbert Asquith; artist George Romney; and Princess Amelia, daughter of George II. Housebuilding began here in 1717, and the view, with its hansoms and carriages, is part of a small run of postcards by stamp dealer William Lincoln of Holles Street.

Great Titchfield Street by Riding House Street, Off Oxford Street, *c.* 1906

While Oxford Street attracted shoppers from afar, Great Titchfield Street, with its street market, catered for a more localised clientele from the surrounding residential streets. In this autochrome postcard by the Pictorial Stationery Co. it is sale time at Lilley & Skinner's, while some fancy ironwork marks the King's Arms pub by Union Street.

Madame Tussaud's, Marylebone Road, *c.* 1906

Madame Marie Tussaud's collection of wax figures were exhibited in Baker Street in 1835 before moving in 1884 to this purpose-built exhibition hall. The enduring popularity of the waxworks has seen the exhibition expand and include other attractions including a cinema in 1909. There would be a new cinema following a fire in 1925 and in 1958 the Planetarium would arise here. Marylebone Road was laid out in 1757 as 'The New Road' – it was London's first northern bypass.

Portland Place, Marylebone, *c.* 1906

When Robert and James Adam began building here in 1776 their new street was the widest in London and the fine town houses the subject of much admiration. In the 1820s, the street was utilised by Nash as the northern part of his Regent Street scheme extending the highway into Regents Park via the exquisite Park Crescent. The preserved terraces within the park itself reveal Nash's work at its more spectacular. In this autochrome postcard the Adam's houses are seen as planned, but their number would diminish later in the twentieth century.

Tottenham Court Road from Oxford Street, 1884

Running northwards from Oxford Street and passing the manor of Tottenhall or Tottenham Court along the way, this was still a road in rural Middlesex in the mid-1700s, but by the end of the century, London's expansion had caught up with it and the street's urban aspect began to take shape. As with many London roads, Tottenham Court Road developed its own character and became colonised by the furniture trade with noted emporia Maple's and Heal's in business alongside smaller retailers. The later twentieth century brought a concentration of shops specialising in the audio-visual and computer trades. Seen to the right of the view is an untypical enterprise for this area, Meux's Horseshoe Brewery, which flourished here from the mid-1700s to the early 1900s before the site was given over to entertainment in the form of the Court cinema (1911) and, from 1930, its grandiose successor the Dominion. The view predates road widening, which would remove the block of shops to the left and tiny Boziers Court, a byway that ran behind them. The wall of the doomed properties gives an insight into London's entertainment options in 1884 with posters advertising a production at the Royal Princess's Theatre, Oxford Street; Grosvenor Gallery's Summer Exhibition, New Bond Street; and the International Exhibition at the Crystal Palace.

This finely detailed lantern slide was photographed from a building whose site would from 1959 be given to the iconic Centre Point – Charing Cross Road would not exist until 1887. The colourist here had made a good job of picturing the smoky haze which hung over Victorian London on windless days.

Eyre Street Hill, Clerkenwell, *c.* 1900

In the nineteenth century, immigrant families from Italy settled in a small area off Clerkenwell Road, bringing with them the colour and customs of their homeland together with the trades and crafts that went with them. Here were ice cream vendors, street performers and musicians together with the craftsmen whose instruments created that most distinctive sound of the Victorian and Edwardian street, the street piano or barrel organ. Eyre Street Hill was the High Street of 'Little Italy' and there are still many reminders of the old community.

St Peter's Church, Clerkenwell Road, *c.* 1908

The focal point for Clerkenwell's Italian community, the church was built in 1863, and from 1883 the Feast of Our Lady of Mount Carmel has been celebrated annually when the statue of the Madonna, which is sacred to the Italians, is carried in procession through the neighbourhood.

Wych Street, Strand, *c.* **1895**

This atmospheric byway arose on part of the site of the Saxon town of Lundenwic, which flourished outside the walls of the Roman city from around AD 600 to AD 850. Although nothing of the Saxon town remains above ground, an air of antiquity clung to this neighbourhood in which a number of centuries-old timber-framed buildings overhung the narrow streets. This lantern slide gives a reminder of Wych Street in its final dilapidated years before clearance and the creation of the spacious streets and noble stone fronted buildings of the new Aldwych/Kingsway, the first major new roads to be built in London in the twentieth century.

Drinking Fountain and Horse Trough, Strand, *c.* **1895**

Throughout the nineteenth century, London's streets were filled with horses and other animals, and the reek of the stables permeated everything. The need for clean drinking water was addressed in 1859 when The Metropolitan Drinking Fountain and Cattle Trough Association was set up to provide 'free supplies of water for man and beast in the streets of London' at a time when the threat of cholera was never far away. Some of the old granite troughs have survived but the one seen here by the church of St Mary-le-Strand (1717) has long gone, as has the cast iron drinking fountain (*c.* 1877) with its Greek influenced classical design. The houses on the left run on into Holywell Street, one of the ancient streets soon to be cleared for the epic Aldwych/Kingsway improvements.

THE OLD GATEWAY, LINCOLN'S INN, W.C.

Middle Temple Hall, *c.* 1897

The Inner and Middle Temple are mellow and ancient enclaves of the legal profession where it is still possible to stroll through gaslit courts and lanes that vividly recall the London of past centuries. Magnificence also abounds: Middle Temple Hall dates from around 1562 and in addition to its role as a members' dining hall, it was also used for plays and other entertainments. Shakespeare's *Twelfth Night* was produced here in 1601. The image comes from a rare early example of a colour-enhanced photograph on an English postcard – artist depictions were more usual in the 1890s.

The Gateway, Lincoln's Inn, Chancery Lane, *c.* 1908

Outside a toffee apple seller attracts the local youth while within is another lawyers' precinct and the venerable architecture for which these old legal inns are renowned. The Gatehouse was built in 1518 and reconstructed in 1969, and through it is a glimpse of Old Hall dating from 1492. The postcard is a Misch & Co. 'Camera Graph'.

Newgate Prison, Newgate Street by Old Bailey, *c.* 1895

Built in 1780 on a site used for a prison since the twelfth century, this was a dreaded place of incarceration for London's ne'er-do-wells and, following the abandonment of public execution at Tyburn in 1783, a place where hangings took place on a scaffold outside Newgate's forbidding walls. This public spectacle continued until 1868 – thereafter the ultimate punishment was administered inside the prison until the closure which preceded demolition in 1902. The site was then taken by the Central Criminal Courts, the Old Bailey, opened by King Edward VII and Queen Alexandra on 27 February 1907. The prison's Old Bailey frontage is caught on this lantern slide as roadworks disrupt the street.

The Royal Courts of Justice, Strand, *c.* 1948

This was one of the more spectacular examples of the Gothic Revival in Victorian London and was built from 1871 to 1882 to replace outmoded facilities, which had been located beside Westminster Hall since 1825. The building, which was designed by G. E. Street, handles cases of civil rather than criminal law and its arrival added another element to 'Legal London', the quarter of legal Inns of Court and Chancery concentrated around the western boundaries of the City of London. This postcard by Raphael Tuck shows how high-quality colour photography allied to improved printing processes was beginning to transform the style of the picture postcard view in the post-war years.

Temple Bar, Fleet Street, c. 1876

In past centuries, the Westminster and City of London boundary was marked by a chain across the road before more ambitious structures culminated in this Wren designed gateway which was put up in the 1670s. As traffic levels grew, Temple Bar was deemed an obstruction and in 1878 it was taken down and later rebuilt in a rural setting at Theobalds Park, Hertfordshire. The gateway was always a popular subject for photographers but by the 1890s when the first picture postcards appeared it had gone. However, Edwardian Londoners still mourning the loss of their historic landmark were able to buy this souvenir version of an earlier image – little realising that a century on, Temple Bar would return to the city on a new site beside St Paul's Cathedral.

Temple Bar from a Window in Pickett Street, Strand, c. 1865

Pickett Street was for some sixty years the north-eastern extremity of the Strand, its name coming from a late eighteenth-century improvement scheme which swept away an ancient and unsavoury quarter of meat traders' shops called Butcher Row. Pickett Street and Pickett Place were themselves cleared away in the 1870s to create a site for the Royal Courts of Justice, the Law Courts. The image from a stereo card also pictures a pair of ancient wooden houses spared by the Great Fire (1666) to house the Wig & Pen Club, a noted haunt of the legal profession.

Old Temple Bar. 1670-1878.

Covent Garden Market, *c.* 1903

Beginning around 1656, London's famous fruit and vegetable market colonised London's first square, an elegant residential creation in the Italian style dating from 1629–37. This autochrome postcard captures a little of the chaos that prevailed in the market through the following centuries before closure and removal to Nine Elms in 1974. This cleared the way for restoration of historic structures and a new life as a quarter of small trendy shops, craft and collectables markets and a lively street life complete with events, buskers and entertainers performing on the piazza.

The Old Curiosity Shop, Portsmouth Street Near Kingsway, *c.* 1918

For over a century, visitors to this quaint relic have been beguiled by tales of its links to the works of Charles Dickens but these remain unproven and unlikely. The building is, however, unique and it probably originated in the seventeenth century as a single cottage in what was then a semi-rural area on the edge of London. A favourite subject for postcards, this one by J. Salmon shows the shop when occupied by waste paper merchant Horace Poole before the sale of Dickensian souvenirs became the principal business.

St Paul's Cathedral, c. 1885

The high point of Ludgate Hill has been crowned by a place of worship dedicated to St Paul since Mellitus, Bishop of London, built the first St Paul's here in AD 604. Norman and medieval cathedrals followed, the latter boasting a mighty 489-foot spire, given additional prominence by the cathedral's elevated site. The spire was felled by lightning in 1561; in 1666, the Great Fire reduced the cathedral to a smouldering ruin clearing the way for Sir Christopher Wren's grand design, which, when finished in 1711, was unlike anything the city had seen before.

Here a pair of lantern slides picture St Paul's when its dominance of the city skyline was total and the intrusions of the twentieth century had yet to arrive. In the upper image the slate and tile roofs of the post-fire city run right up to the cathedral, while in the picture to the right modest buildings frame the view as seen from Cheapside. This view also shows the book publisher's heartland of Paternoster Row and Nicholson's department store, which would be rebuilt in grander style in 1900.

Cheapside from St Paul's Churchyard, *c.* 1890

In medieval London this was Westchepe, the city's principal market place, a colourful and thriving *mélange* of shoppers, traders and animals in the then densely populated City of London. At its centre, in a street far wider than the one we know today, was Chepe Cross, another of the Eleanor Crosses set up to mark the resting places of Queen Eleanor's funeral cortège on its way to Westminster Abbey in 1290. At its western end was the dominating presence of old St Paul's and there were several ancient churches along the way, including the eleventh-century St Mary-le-Bow. Cheapside was also an important east/west highway between Westminster and the Tower of London, and at times of national rejoicing or sorrow the street witnessed grand processions and there were jousting tournaments. Cheapside's wooden houses succumbed to the Great Fire in 1666 as did its churches and cathedral, but a new Cheapside arose from the ashes together with a fine new St Mary-le-Bow, built to Wren's designs. Many relics of the church's true antiquity may still be seen in the crypt. By Victorian times, the building line had encroached into the formerly spacious street, narrowing it, but it maintained its position as the City of London's premier shopping street, as may be seen on this lantern slide, the work of Cheapside photographer George Edward Wood. The distant greenery is a venerable Plane tree marking the churchyard of the twelfth-century St Peter Westchepe, which was not rebuilt after the Great Fire. Much of Cheapside was reduced to rubble in the Second World War, but post-war planners have not dealt kindly with the street and there is little in the bland office blocks to celebrate the glories of Cheapside in past centuries.

Remarkably there were once around 100 churches in the square mile of the City of London, all serving tiny but populous parishes where overcrowding was rife but the sanctuary of an ancient church was always close at hand. Many of the churches were rebuilt by Wren and his contemporaries after the Great Fire; later on, as the great financial powerhouse of the city took shape and the resident population declined in the face of rising site values, some of the churches were edged out while war damage accounted for others. The churches still standing a century ago were popular subjects for the postcard publishers of the day.

Left: St Augustine, Austin Friars – the church founded in 1253 survived the fire but not the Blitz. It was rebuilt in 1954. Centre: St Magnus-the-Martyr, Lower Thames Street, by Wren c. 1684. Right: St Giles Cripplegate. The medieval church is seen above a bastion on the Roman city wall in what is now the Barbican Estate (1963).

The Bank of England, *c. 1895*

The Bank has been on its site in Threadneedle Street since 1734 – it was reconstructed from 1788–1827 to the condition seen here. The years 1921–39 would see the old low-rise Bank transformed by new building within the preserved perimeter walls, resulting in the grandiose Bank we know today. This lantern slide has preserved a lively slice of city life with everyone rushing about their business and a pair of policemen endeavouring to control the eternal traffic.

The Royal Exchange and Bank of England, *c. 1920*

Founded in 1566 as a business meeting-place for city merchants by Sir Thomas Gresham, the Exchange has undergone a series of rebuildings, the last of which in 1844 resulted in the neoclassical landmark we see here in the financial heart of the city. This Salmon postcard captures a city mood: one of those gloomy days when all seems grey apart from the red liveries of the buses.

Wash House Court, Charterhouse, c. 1907

Among the joys of London are its hidden and often overlooked corners, tranquil and historic oases often within yards of thunderous main roads. Among them is Charterhouse, which was founded in 1371 as a Carthusian Priory before the complex of buildings took on a new role as a public school – this moved away in 1872. There were also almshouses for pensioners or 'brothers' who continue to be cared for here. The postcard by E. Bottom & Co. shows the age-blackened stones of Wash House Court where lay brothers had quarters in the sixteenth century.

The Monument, c. 1905

The City of London's greatest calamity, the Great Fire of 1666, destroyed around four fifths of the medieval city, but out of the ruins arose a new city and the Monument in commemoration of the disaster. Designed by Wren and his associate Robert Hooke, the column of Portland stones rises 202 feet, this being the distance from the seat of the fire, Farynor's bakery in Pudding Lane. It took a 3d entry fee, 311 steps and a robust pair of lungs to reach the Monument's viewing gallery, but the grand panorama then revealed was equally breathtaking.

THE MARKET HALL. HARRODS.

London Shopping – Harrod's, Brompton Road, *c.* 1906

London is an internationally renowned shopping city with a bewildering choice of retail outlets ranging from its palatial West End department stores, through countless local shopping parades and specialist stores to lively street markets thronged with bargain hunters. Harrod's is one of the more opulent of the great department stores, but it all began in a modest way in 1848 when Charles Henry Harrod set up a grocery shop in a then far from fashionable part of town. Decades of successful trading and prosperity brought Harrod's the means to build a spectacular terracotta fronted store, which arose in Brompton Road from 1901–05. Soon after completion of the rebuilding, Harrod's could boast its own set of six Oilette postcards – this one displays the fine Doulton tiling in the food halls.

Selfridge's, Oxford Street, *c.* 1913

Having made his fortune in Chicago, American entrepreneur Gordon Selfridge cleverly secured the longest unbroken frontage on to London's premier shopping street for his London store, the first part of which opened in 1909. As is seen here, Selfridge's first occupied premises on both sides of the street until its frontage was finally completed. This postcard advertisement imagines a Zeppelin's view of the store at a time when these airships represented the ultimate in luxury air travel. Tragically, the First World War was imminent and the word Zeppelin would soon be one of terror as the airships began their bombing raids in 1915.

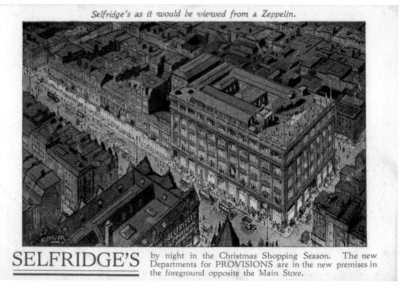

Selfridge's as it would be viewed from a Zeppelin.

SELFRIDGE'S by night in the Christmas Shopping Season. The new Departments for PROVISIONS are in the new premises in the foreground opposite the Main Store.

Lambert & Co., Gold and Silversmiths, Coventry Street, Near Piccadilly Circus, c. 1865
Established in 1803, the shop proudly displays its Royal Warrant and an enticing array of stock set behind a Georgian shopfront featuring the typical small square windowpanes of that era. Remarkably, the old shop would survive, little changed into the 1910s, but demolition around 1914 would remove the last shop of its type in the West End. Arundell Street, left, would also vanish together with tiny Panton Square, which lay at the end of it. Part of the Trocadero complex now covers the site. The image comes from a *carte-de-visite,* which would have been handed out to publicise the shop.

Page & Shaw, Confectioners, 68 Piccadilly by Dover Street, c. 1922
Luxury shopping has traditionally been concentrated in the West End where streets of smart and exclusive emporia have long tempted the well-heeled into parting with their guineas. Here the Moorish shopfront is a prelude to the delights within for a company that also had branches in Kensington and the Strand.

Warwick St. Westminster.

THE PROBLEM SOLVED!

Warwick Street (Now Warwick Way), Westminster, *c.* 1905

Serving northern Pimlico and southern Belgravia, this is an example of the shopping parades, which provide day-to-day domestic essentials for local communities throughout London. This one is still thriving but the market stalls and barrows have had to make room for car parking. The 1900s was the first decade in which postcards of local streets like this were available; they were usually in sepia monochrome, coloured ones being less frequently produced.

The London Pure Milk Association, 4 Eccleston Street, Belgravia, *c.* 1909

The traditional method of delivering milk in Victorian and Edwardian London was from a churn mounted on a handcart – the householder would provide a receptacle, which would be filled direct from the churn. In an effort to improve hygiene and efficiency, milk bottles were introduced into this country in 1906, the company shown here being one of the first to adopt the new system. It cost 4*d* per quart (two pints) and there were two deliveries per day via an 'Insulated Ice Delivery Car' or the milk could be collected from the company's shops. Aluminium caps for milk bottles appeared in 1929 and electric milk floats arrived in 1932. The old Eccleston Street shopfront can still be seen, but the dairy has long departed.

Carnaby Street, 1960s

London's 'Swinging Sixties' witnessed the transformation of a drab Soho backstreet into a colourful extravaganza of teenage fashion and psychedelic art, a place where the trendy young things of the day crowded the bright music-filled boutiques for the latest 'gear'. Here a commercial postcard by Judge's of Hastings and a pair of visitor's snapshots capture something of the atmosphere of Carnaby Street's early days. Half a century on, the street retains its allure as one of London's specialist shopping streets. (*Top left image by courtesy of Judge's Postcards, Hastings*)

Leather Lane Market, Holborn, *c.* 1895

Some dating back many centuries, London's street markets offer a vibrant slice of Cockney street life with bargain seekers and banter in abundance. Leather Lane originated in the thirteenth century as a rural byway which by the seventeenth century was being built up, attracting outdoor traders. In Victorian times, this was an area of severe poverty and the market was beset by beggars and thieves, but modern times have seen a revitalisation here with lunchtime shoppers from the area's new office blocks.

Wentworth Street Market, Whitechapel, *c.* 1895

An amateur photographer's lantern slide pictures a busy day in this tributary of the world-famous Petticoat Lane market in London's inner East End.

An East End Market.

Clockwise from Top Left:

Petticoat Lane Market, *c*. 1918

The market has been flavoured through three centuries by settlers from other lands, while the ever present Cockney traders mark this as the archetypal East End market. This Celesque postcard pictures the market when Jewish traders predominated.

Brick Lane Market, *c*. 1906

Brick Lane is a classic example of how a street can change and adapt to suit the needs of different ethnic groups who settle around it. French Huguenots were here from the late seventeenth century leaving a legacy of fine town houses, while Jewish refugees made the street their own from the 1880s, complete with synagogues and beigel shops. Today, it is the High Street of 'Banglatown' with a colourful Asian community, vibrant with aromatic restaurants and bright fabric shops.

The Market, Morgan Buildings, Hessel Street, Whitechapel, *c*. 1905

A small off-street market, which served a poor Jewish neighbourhood off Commercial Road.

Clockwise from Top Left:

Soho Markets in the 1960s: Rupert Street Near Archer Street

A haunt of artists and writers, a centre of nightlife and theatre-going, and a locality of diverse populations nurtured by a profusion of Continental restaurants, Soho has always seemed a place apart from the London flow, yet its street markets are firmly set in the London tradition. The diversity of Rupert Street is caught here with L. Viazzani's sandwich shop on the left and a branch of the once prolific Home & Colonial stores at the end of the row by Brewer Street.

Rupert Street by Tisbury Court with Shaftesbury Avenue in the Distance

Berwick Street Market

While Rupert Street's stalls have declined in the present day, Berwick Street remains a popular and vibrant local market. The market's origins can be traced back to the 1700s.

Wholesale Markets: Borough Market, Southwark, *c.* 1906

This fruit and vegetable market has an ancestry that can be traced back to the thirteenth century but the buildings here now were put up from 1851. With volcanic sounds from the overhead railway lines, Borough Market retains an abundance of Victorian atmosphere in its more recent incarnation as a gourmet food market.

Smithfield Market

In the twelfth century, a horse fair was held on the 'smooth field' on the edge of the City of London, and in 1638, a cattle market was established. This was relocated to Islington in 1855, following which the buildings for the meat market we know today were erected, opening in 1868. The frontage on to Charterhouse Street is seen on a locally published postcard from 1906, left, while a Celesque postcard, far right, pictures a 'bummaree', a market porter, with a crippled child a poignant presence in the background.

London Characters: the Costermonger, Trafalgar Square, c. 1913

A century ago, London's streets were still enriched by an army of vendors, hawkers, itinerant traders and those providing services of various kinds to the passer-by. Here a costermonger plies his trade in the grand setting of Trafalgar Square against a backdrop of St Martin-in-the-Fields with two ladies from London's Italian community completing their purchases. The image comes from a series of around 100 'London Life' postcards by the Rotary Photographic Co. Ltd, most of which are in monochrome, but this is one of a small number reissued as a 'hand-painted real photograph'. Always a popular theme for the early postcard album, 'London Life' cards by a variety of publishers have left a fine pictorial legacy of the characters who once enlivened London's streets.

LONDON LIFE. CITY FRUIT HAWKER.

10513-F

Ice Cream Vendors: Whitechapel High Street, *c.* 1895 (Above), and Hackney Downs Station, *c.* 1913 (Left)

The street sales of ice cream in Victorian London was the province of Italian 'hokey-pokey' men who dispensed their 'pure ices' in glasses or cups as seen in the image from a Victorian lantern slide. By the time the Rotary postcard, left, was published, ice cream wafers had been introduced and the vendor is seen with his 'slide', which was used to create the icy sandwich. Although new-style cones had been introduced around 1910, these youths seem happy enough with their treats in old-style glasses.

Preparing for the Paper Round, Sherwood Street, Soho, c. 1904

Staff from a newsagent's shop in Sherwood Street prepare for the deliveries in a street, which was then lined with shops. The Regent Palace Hotel (1915) and the Piccadilly Theatre (1928) would replace them.

Spreading the Word:

Newsboy, City of London, c. 1913

Boys selling newspapers in the street have joined the ranks of London's lost tribes, but this one's lurid headline would have helped to sell a few more copies.

Sandwich Board Man, Trafalgar Square, c. 1913

A popular way of imparting information, and one that endures in the present day.

LONDON LIFE. SANDWICH BOARD MAN.

10514-

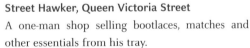

Street Hawker, Queen Victoria Street

A one-man shop selling bootlaces, matches and other essentials from his tray.

Covent Garden Market Porter

A tradition grew up among the porters to attempt to carry as much as possible on their heads, as seen here. In the background, the pedimented building with the large lunette was part of the Flower Market – it would house the London Transport Museum from 1980. To the left is the site of a Turkish bath, which opened in 1683.

Pavement Artist, Victoria Embankment

Popular characters who maintain a presence in modern London. These Celesque postcards come from a set of 'London Types', *c.* 1913.

Street Musicians

Among the sounds heard in Victorian and Edwardian London, those produced by an army of performers was never far away and not always welcomed by those living in quiet residential streets. Italian immigrant organ grinders and hurdy-gurdy men were a prolific breed and could be seen and heard in many parts of town. The gentleman in the right-hand picture has attracted the usual youthful followers as he operates his street organ in Ogle Street, Marylebone, against a backdrop of St Charles' Roman Catholic church (1862), while the elderly player in the Oilette postcard has this unidentified location to himself. Animals were sometimes employed as part of the act, as seen in the youthful performance, lower left.

"With best love.
Little Red Riding Hood."

"Postage 2½d."

The Royal Mail in Edwardian London

Despite this modern age of electronic communication, the ritual of posting letters endures, as does the role of the postman. These postcard scenes from a century ago are from Islington, top left; the City of London, lower left; and the right-hand image is from Southwark. The first pillar boxes in London were put up in 1855 and all of them were painted red from 1874.

Making Artificial Flowers at the Crippleage, Sekforde Street, Clerkenwell, c. 1914

Philanthropist John Groom, the 7th Earl of Shaftesbury, founded the Watercress and Flowergirl Christian Mission in 1866 as a charity to care for and give work training to disabled girls up to the age of fifteen. The charity remained in Clerkenwell into the 1930s, and there was a John Groom orphanage for girls at Clacton-on-Sea.

Dr Barnardo's Homes, Stepney Causeway, c. 1910

Dublin born Thomas Barnardo devoted his life to the protection and education of the multitude of homeless children in the poverty stricken neighbourhoods of the old East End and opened his first lodging house for them in Stepney Causeway in 1870. The children were taught a variety of skills and crafts to prepare them for life outside the homes, the blacksmith shop seen here being one example of the training available. As ever, sets of postcards depict this aspect of life in London.

XMAS MORN.
MESSENGER DELIVERING PRESENTS

DISTRICT MESSENGERS RESERVING PLACES AT THE THEATRE

District Messengers, *c.* 1906

The District Messengers were a large corps of smartly uniformed youths (and a few girls) who were employed to perform a variety of useful tasks around town. These included baby walking, general deliveries (top left) and reserving places in theatre queues (right). A set of six Oilette cards highlight their work.

Children in a London Street, *c.* 1900

In this lantern slide these youngsters appear to be recreating characters from earlier times, including a barefoot flower girl and a boy crossing sweeper, also barefoot. These were some of the tasks undertaken by children in poor areas of Victorian London.

**Arts, Entertainment and Events: The Royal Albert Hall,
Kensington Gore, *c.* 1875**

The Great Exhibition of 1851 was held in Hyde Park and housed
in Sir Joseph Paxton's glass fantasy, Crystal Palace, where
it generated enough profit to allow a large area of land to
the south of Kensington Gardens to be purchased for the
establishment of a cultural quarter of museums, institutions
and colleges. An early manifestation of this came in 1862
with the staging of the International Exhibition in South
Kensington, while in 1867 a grand concert hall began to
take shape in Kensington Gore. The foundation stone of
the Royal Albert Hall of Arts and Sciences was laid by
Queen Victoria and the hall was named in honour of the
late Prince Albert, the Queen's Consort who had overseen
the 1851 exhibition. Completed in 1871, the Albert Hall went
on to become a much-loved concert venue, and following the
wartime destruction of the Queen's Hall, Langham Place, it
began to stage the Henry Wood Promenade Concerts, The Proms,
which have been held here annually ever since. This lantern slide
pictures the Albert Hall in the first decade of its life and before
the arrival of Albert Hall Mansions, the blocks of mansion flats from
1880–87, which would set a new trend in flat design in London.

The International Exhibition, Cromwell Road and Exhibition Road, South Kensington, 1862

This vast event was opened by the Duke of Cambridge on 1 May 1862 and was remarkable for the range and diversity of its exhibits, which reflected the latest technology and progress in the Industrial Revolution. The event lasted until 1 November 1862 but the elaborate building was not used again, with demolition clearing the way for the Natural History Museum in 1881. Left: The eastern dome and entrance, Exhibition Road. Centre: Thomas Minton's Majolica ware fountain whose perfumed waters gave a cooling effect in a building that overheated in the London summer. Right: The nave, showing the congested displays and the galleries crammed with yet more exhibits. The images are by the London Stereoscopic and Photographic Company.

The Gigantic Wheel, Earls Court Exhibition Grounds, *c.* 1905

The London Eye, the spectacular observation wheel, has become an icon of modern London, but over a century earlier it was possible to enjoy a similar experience in west London. From 1894, the Earls Court Exhibition and Pleasure Grounds boasted a mighty wheel, 300 foot in diameter and modelled on the great Ferris wheel at the World's Fair in Chicago. The twenty-minute ride offered a breathtaking panorama of London, and in what was still a low-rise city, the wheel itself was a dramatic sight from many parts of the capital.

Topsy Turvey House, an Earls Court Exhibit in 1902

Earls Court was popular resort created on spare railway land at the boundary of Kensington and Fulham where it staged a new exhibition annually until 1914 when its halls were used as a refugee camp for Belgian people displaced by the First World War. Earls Court endures as an exhibition and conference venue with new halls dating from 1937 and 1991.

The Festival of Britain, South Bank, Lambeth, 1951

Battered by years of war, dereliction and austerity, the 1940s was London's darkest decade, but with the 1950s came a new sense of optimism and a morale-boosting exhibition at three sites in London: the South Bank, Battersea Park and Poplar where new trends in architecture were showcased. The view here looks along the formerly industrialised Belvedere Road and shows the festival's only permanent building, the Royal Festival Hall; beyond is the prominent Dome of Discovery and the aluminium needle which is the Skylon. Also seen is the railway viaduct, which bisects the festival site, its grim bricks suitably tarted-up for the occasion.

The Crossway, Festival of Britain, South Bank, 1951

The festival introduced Londoners to a bright and colourful style of modern architecture and attractive open-air restaurants where the summery weather could be appreciated in a Thames-side area opened for public use for the first time. These are two of the colourful postcards that visitors posted in some quantity from the Festival Post Office.

Entrance to the Fun Fair, Battersea Park, *c.* 1960

The Fun Fair and adjacent pleasure grounds were laid out for the Festival of Britain in 1951 providing attractions that lasted until the Fun Fair closed in 1972. Popular rides included a large wood-framed big dipper and a Ferris wheel, while many of the usual diversions of a traditional English fairground were also featured. There was also a children's zoo and the iconic Emmett Railway, while the larger site contained a perfumed grotto, spectacular water features, and the Tree Walk from which this photograph was taken.

Cremorne Gardens, Chelsea, *c.* 1860

A century earlier, Cremorne existed as a public pleasure ground from 1845 to 1877 and featured fountains, grottoes, and leafy pathways. There was also a Thames-side maze, a marionette theatre, and a bowling saloon to popularise the resort. Following closure, the Cremorne site was intensively built up with a grid of new streets, all of which suffered from pollution from Lots Road Power Station, which was built from 1902–05 on part of the Cremorne grounds – it provided electricity for the Underground. The lost beauty of old Cremorne is caught on this stereoscopic card.

Queen Victoria's Diamond Jubilee, June 1897

Londoners invariably embrace great royal events with patriotic enthusiasm, and when Queen Victoria celebrated the Golden Jubilee of her reign in 1887 and her Diamond Jubilee in 1897 the capital responded in the traditional manner with lavishly decorated streets. On the day of her Diamond Jubilee, the Queen attended a service of thanksgiving at St Paul's Cathedral and, accompanied by a colourful military procession on the outward and return journeys to Buckingham Palace, was greeted by well-wishers thronging the streets to catch a glimpse of the much-loved monarch in her carriage. These photographs were taken on part of the processional route, St James's Street, which is at the heart of an aristocratic area of grand town houses and gentlemen's clubs. Both the glass-lantern slide (left) and stereoscopic photograph,(right) show the extravagant garlanding in the street.

Silver Jubilee Decorations, Oxford Circus, 1935

King George V and Queen Mary were crowned in Westminster Abbey on 22 June 1911 and to national rejoicing celebrated their Silver Jubilee in 1935. To mark the occasion, Raphael Tuck & Sons, the publishers of high-quality postcards since 1900 issued a set of six cards reproduced 'from photographs taken in actual colour', an early example of a process which would soon become commonplace. This card from the set pictures an eastward looking view along Oxford Street with its grand department stores on the sunny south-facing side of the street, left.

Coronation Decorations, Fleet Street, 1902

The twentieth century soon brought a new monarch and the dawn of the Edwardian era with the coronation of King Edward VII and Queen Alexandra in Westminster Abbey on 9 August 1902. In common with many London streets, Fleet Street was adorned with patriotic displays, while the unsightly railway bridge at Ludgate Hill was made glorious by colourful decorations.

Coronation Decorations, the Pavilion Archway, Kensington Road, Summer, 1953
The coronation of Queen Elizabeth II took place on a rainy 2 June 1953 and, as ever, the nation celebrated with street parties and decorations while London filled with visitors anxious to witness the historic occasion. Here an amateur photographer's glass slide pictures an elaborate construction of banners and pennants designed to recall the tournament pavilions of the first Elizabethan age (1558–1603). The archway was designed as a spectacular entry point to the Royal Borough of Kensington at coronation time and was located close to Kensington Palace where Queen Victoria spent her childhood years.

Coronation Decorations, The Dorchester, Park Lane, 1953
This famous hotel, which had opened in 1931, celebrated the Queen's coronation with a colourful display designed by Oliver Messel, who had also designed suites within the hotel.

The Royal Alhambra Palace, Leicester Square, c. 1870

This country's largest concentration of theatres graces a swathe of the West End from St James's to Holborn with Leicester Square a particular focus of the entertainment industry. From 1854 to 1936 Leicester Square's eastern side was dominated by the Alhambra with its Moorish style architecture – it was a building where Londoners came at various times to savour the delights of circus, music hall, lavish ballets and stage shows.

In the early years of its life, however, the building was not a theatre at all but an exhibition hall called The Royal Panopticon of Science and Art, but this failed to attract enough visitors to remain viable. The old landmark was finally demolished in 1936 and in its place arose a modern icon of the cinema age, the Odeon, Leicester Square, with its eye-catching façade and tower in black granite. A stereoscopic photograph from the cab rank on the west side of the square.

The Alhambra, London.

The Alhambra, c. 1906

Films would sometimes be shown during variety programmes, but Leicester Square's first purpose-built cinema would soon open in the building at the far right of this British Mirror postcard view (see page 78).

In Edwardian times popular actors and actresses were the celebrities of the day with many families' postcard albums featuring a selection of their photographs, while the theatres in which they performed were also in demand. The 'EFA London Theatre' series of cards pictured many well-known West End venues in a colourful set based on original photographs, and here are three of them.

Left: Daly's Theatre, Cranbourn Street (1893–1937) – the Warner Cinema would take the site.

Centre: The Tivoli, Strand (1890–1914).

Right: Lyric Theatre (1888) and the Apollo Theatre (1901), which are adjoining theatres in Shaftesbury Avenue that are still flourishing.

St James's Theatre, King Street from Bury Street, St James's, *c.* 1906
Dating from 1835, this beautiful theatre staged the first production of Oscar Wilde's *Lady Windermere's Fan* (1892) and *The Importance of Being Earnest* (1895), and from 1950–54 the management of Laurence Olivier and Vivien Leigh staged productions of Shakespeare and Tyrone Guthrie among others. The streetscape would be the poorer for the loss of this fine building upon its closure in 1957.

The New Gaiety Theatre, Strand, *c.* 1905
The original Gaiety Theatre (1868) gave its site in the Aldwych scheme, one of the first flowerings of which was the New Gaiety Theatre, which opened on 26 October 1903. Among theatrical legends to tread its boards were Leslie Henson, Cecily Courtneidge and Jack Hulbert, but in 1957 it became another London theatre to suffer closure.

The New Egyptian Hall
170 Piccadilly (opposite Bond St)

The New Egyptian Hall
Cinematograph Tea Rooms

The Circle in the Square Cinema, Leicester Square, *c.* 1910

Leicester Square boasts grand and glamorous cinemas on three of its sides and is renowned for its glitzy film premieres, but a century ago the Square's first real cinema was a spartan affair with bare light bulbs and hard seating for 198 patrons.

The Circle in the Square opened on 5 June 1909 and was promoted as 'London's Leading Bioscopic Display' and, as usual, there was a tea room. The cinema was renamed Cupid's in 1914 and Palm Court Cinema in 1926, but the advent of talking pictures at the Empire, Leicester Square, killed the old place off by 1928.

The New Egyptian Hall, Piccadilly, *c.* 1908

London's West End is at the forefront of the cinema industry and can claim a lengthy ancestry from Victorian times when the first flickering 'animated photographs' were demonstrated to enthralled audiences. The Egyptian Hall began showing films in 1896 as part of a varied programme of entertainment and following rebuilding as the New Egyptian Hall in 1907 it became a proper cinema with 123 seats and a pretty tea room in the Japanese style. It lasted until 1912.

The Empire, High Road, Balham, *c.* 1907

The Empire, High Road, Balham, *c.* 1907

As the Edwardian decade progressed, displays of 'living pictures' evolved from variety show and fairground novelties into a popular new entertainment medium housed in dedicated viewing halls – the first cinemas. These spread throughout London and elsewhere, and this new facility in suburban Balham was a typical example.

'Kinoplastikon', Scala Theatre, Charlotte Street, Fitzrovia, *c.* 1911

Increasing sophistication brought more luxurious cinemas and innovative presentations, one of the most ambitious being a German idea called 'Kinoplastikon', which combined pseudo-stereoscopic films shown in colour with stage props and a musical accompaniment by gramophone. This and other colour shows at the Scala were popular and complex but the advent of the First World War brought about their closure. This poster-style postcard depicting a fashionably dressed audience is not a photograph but its theme of colour cinematography renders its inclusion appropriate.

Piccadilly Circus, *c.* 1923

When Piccadilly Circus entered the twentieth century the street was demurely lit by gas lamps but before many years had elapsed increasing sophistication in lighting had transformed the Circus into an electrical wonderland. The façade of Piccadilly Mansions, left, which curves round into Shaftesbury Avenue, was an early focus for ambitious electrical advertising displays but the Circus had to wait until 1924 for its first neon sign, although Coventry Street had one in 1913. This anonymously published postcard catches some 1920s atmosphere and the famous 'Bovril' and 'Schweppes' signs which endured for several decades. The London Pavilion highlights its current production, right.

A Wet Night in the West End – Leicester Square from Coventry Street, *c.* 1938

In the years leading up to the Second World War, electric advertising spread into formerly sober localities like Trafalgar Square and Ludgate Circus, while at the centre of London's nightlife, the signs blazed ever more brightly. This snapshot catches the neon-lit Monseigneur News Theatre, left, where programmes of cartoons and newsreels were popular in the days before everyone had access to television news. The giant 'Ediswan' sign rises above Leicester Corner, a popular restaurant, while the Coney Island amusement arcade next door provides the usual penny-in-the-slot temptations.

Rupert Street, Soho, 1960s

Soho's fame as a quarter of specialist food shops, exotic restaurants and spirited nightlife is worldwide. Various populations from many lands and through many generations have created the area's unique 'foreign' atmosphere, a process that began in the seventeenth century when Greek Christians and French Huguenots moved in. The most recent arrivals have been the Chinese who at the time of this photograph were beginning to colonise the locality around Gerrard Street following the decline of London's original Chinatown in Limehouse. Rupert Street was not at the centre of the new community but the Hong Kong Emporium (centre of picture) was an early

example of the 'oriental food dealers' to set up in Soho having been here since the 1950s. Restaurants are everywhere in Soho and on view here is Isow's, a popular Jewish restaurant on the Brewer Street/Walker's Court corner. Also here is the Raymond Revuebar, a popular club specialising in gentlemen's entertainment that began life in 1958. An amateur's snapshot captures the bustle of Soho life in Rupert Street's market.

Gennaro's, New Compton Street, by Stacey Street, St Giles, *c.* 1928

Although this restaurant lay outside Soho's boundaries, it was a good example of the type of establishment that reinforced the Continental atmosphere in the side streets of the old West End. Gennaro's prospered under the management of the Sanseverino brothers who went on to acquire the adjoining premises to give a triple frontage. Old Compton Street, Soho, and New Compton Street once faced each other across Charing Cross Road but post-war rebuilding altered the street pattern and the connection was broken.

George Alexander's Cocoa and Coffee Rooms, Lower Thames Street by Botolph Lane, Billingsgate, *c.* 1900

By contrast, establishments like this were found throughout London, often in less affluent areas and those with large working populations. The location here is by Billingsgate, London's wholesale fish market and a good source of customers for the café. The photograph comes from a small album compiled by local stationer, photographer and postcard publisher Joseph Neil who had a shop close by in St Dunstan's Hill.

Janke Bros.
Restaurants and Bakeries.
Tysoe Street, Rosebery Avenue, LONDON E. C.

Janke's Restaurant and Bakery, Tysoe Street, Clerkenwell, c. 1903

In the late 1890s, the pictorial postcard gained in popularity as a means of advertising a product or business, the 'mail shot' of the day. London restaurants and hotels were quick to appreciate the effectiveness of the new medium, many employing artists to create a flattering image, while others, as here, relied on photography and hand tinting to illustrate what was on offer. This attractively designed example spread the word for the Janke brothers, bakers, who specialised in Bride cakes, but in a link with the present day also sold Hovis bread. Janke's restaurant appears a little spartan in this view, but there would have been tempting Continental-style patisserie on offer. The Jankes had a second shop in Old Street, Finsbury and there was a bread delivery service.

Refreshment Rooms, Victoria Buildings, The Façade, Opposite Victoria Station, c. 1910

Another promotional postcard announces the arrival of a new amenity for Victoria's travellers, a tea and dining room in the classic English tradition. With its tempting window displays and Art Nouveau detailing, it was the latest venture for J. P. Restaurants Ltd who had other outlets in London.

LONDON'S LATEST Refreshment Rooms—3 VICTORIA BUILDINGS, opposite Victoria Station (S.E. & C.R.)

Lyon's Corner House, Coventry Street by Rupert Street, Soho, *c.* 1910
Catering chains flourished in earlier decades as they do today, and from the 1890s, one of the more commonly seen names was that of J. Lyons & Co. Ltd., 'Joe Lyons' to generations of Londoners. With competitively priced menus, Lyons catered on a massive scale – the Coventry Street premises (1907) would be extended to seat 4,500 diners by 1923, while the more modest Lyons' tea shops became familiar throughout London.

The Terrace, Piccadilly Hotel, *c.* 1908
Continental-style outdoor dining has become increasingly popular in the modern era but a century ago such facilities were for the most part limited to those found in open spaces rather than busy streets. For the more urban and opulent experience, the Piccadilly Hotel had a beautiful terrace located high above the clamour of Piccadilly's traffic and separated from it by an elegant colonnade. The Piccadilly Hotel had just been completed when photographed for this card. The building is more familiar now as Le Meridien Piccadilly.

The Gaiety Restaurant, Aldwych, *c.* 1906

Opulence abounded in central London for those who could afford it, but not every venture was a success and this restaurant, which adjoined the theatre of the same name, only lasted from 1904 to 1908. The restaurant was another part of the J. Lyons' empire but was considered too large for its location to remain viable.

The Entrance Hall and Stairs, The Trocadero Restaurant, Shaftesbury Avenue, Soho, *c.* 1909

A successor to the Trocadero Palace Music Hall (1882–94), the restaurant was also under the management of J. Lyons and was a fine example of late Victorian extravagance. This photochrome postcard with its gold highlights is also an extravagant affair and pictures part of the Trocadero's remarkable frieze, which was some 90 feet in length.

Wartime, The Blitz, St Andrew's Street, Holborn, *c.* 1941

After two decades of peace, the flow of life in London changed forever with the advent of the Second World War and the air raids that brought terror from above. Few areas escaped the onslaught, and when it was over in 1945, bombsites and dereliction were everywhere with some neighbourhoods losing all their buildings. This photograph captures the horror of Blitzkreig, 'lightning war', in the streets of Holborn where incendiary bombs have sparked blazes against which firefighters can do little.

PLEASE HELP THE HOSPITAL FOR SICK CHILDREN, WHICH IS WITHIN A MILE OF ST. PAUL'S. IT HAS BEEN BOMBED, BUT COME WHAT MAY, WE INTEND TO CARRY ON.
The Hospital for Sick Children, Great Ormond Street, London, W.C. 1.

Great Ormond Street Appeal Postcard, *c.* 1945

London's hospitals performed heroically amid impossible wartime conditions, not least the renowned Hospital for Sick Children, Great Ormond Street, Holborn, which itself suffered bomb damage. Utilising one of the iconic photographs of St Paul's Cathedral amid the fires of the burning city, the hospital's Special Appeals Office issued this postcard to highlight the hospital's plight in its cruellest hour.

Piccadilly Circus in Wartime, *c.* 1943

Wartime blackout restrictions have darkened the famous electric advertisements and alongside the old Guinness and Bovril signs are new appeals for service charities, including an exhibition for the Merchant Navy Comforts Service. There is also an offer of 'Free Insurance for Fire Watchers', a civilian force which saved much property through their vigilance during air raids. The photograph looks along Shaftesbury Avenue, but the Circus's most famous 'resident', the Eros statue, had, in common with some other Londoners, been evacuated to a safer place for the duration of the war.

Bombsites Around St Paul's Cathedral, Cannon Street, *c.* 1950

Empty sites and ruined buildings were familiar features of the London scene for many years following the end of the war. St Paul's Cathedral itself stood firm as destruction raged all around it, but new views of the cathedral were opened up, some of which were preserved as gardens on the old bombsites.

Transport in London: Baker Street Station, Marylebone Road, c. 1908

London's transport system is as vast, complex and labyrinthine as the city itself, but London existed for many centuries before any form of public transportation became available. Although there were coaches for hire as early as 1620, Londoners had to wait until 1829 for their first buses, 1836 for their first railway, 1861 for the first trams and 1863 for the first Underground line. This was the Metropolitan Railway, which, when the first section from Paddington (Bishop's Road) to Farringdon Street on the edge of the City of London opened on 10 January 1863, was a truly pioneering venture, being the world's first subterranean city railway. In spite of the soot and smoke from the steam locomotives, Londoners embraced the new railway with enthusiasm as cross-town journey times were much reduced, and it was not long before extensions and new lines expanded the system into one of the world's great urban railways. Baker Street station was on the Metropolitan Railway original line, and when photographed for an attractive set of locally published view cards it had already become a multi-line facility with interchanges for the Inner Circle and Hammersmith &

Baker St Station.

City services, while from Upper Baker Street there was a separate access to one of the new deep-level tube railways, the Baker Street & Waterloo Railway, the Bakerloo Line. On view here is on one of the station's early entrances, which had been erected in the front gardens of the residential terrace behind it. A new entrance would arrive in 1911 and in 1927, and the rest of the houses would be replaced by a large complex of flats called Chiltern Court.

South Kensington Station

South Kensington Station, *c.* 1907

The 1890s and 1900s brought continuing refinements to the expanding Underground and included the introduction of deep-level electric tube railways, which would have seemed like a true taste of the future for the average Londoner. South Kensington had originally opened on 24 December 1868 as a temporary terminus on a branch line of the Metropolitan Railway, but on 8 January 1907, tube trains on the Great Northern, Piccadilly & Brompton Railway (later the Piccadilly line) began stopping there. In common with other Edwardian tube stations, South Kensington's rebuilt exterior was faced in ox-blood faience tiling, as is shown to striking effect on this local view card, which also pictures the construction of a small shopping arcade, left.

Belsize Park Station, Haverstock Hill, *c.* 1908

The new electric tube lines pushed deeper into London's suburbs, this one on the Charing Cross, Edgware & Hampstead Railway (later a branch of the Northern line) opened on 22 June 1907. The northern terminus of the line was then Golders Green; to the south distant Morden would eventually be reached in 1926 via the longest tunnel on the Underground.

Tube Station. Haverstock Hill

GREAT NORTHERN, PICCADILLY & BROMPTON Ry. PICCADILLY CIRCUS STATION.

The Great Northern, Piccadilly & Brompton Railway (Piccadilly Line), *c.* **1907**
This pair of postcards is from a set published by the railway company to promote 'London's Latest Tube', a service running from Hammersmith to Finsbury Park for which, the cards inform us, 'supplies the long felt want of a connecting link between the west and north of London'. When the first part of the line opened on 15 December 1906, it was the longest of the tubes; it is now the central section of the Piccadilly line which runs from Cockfosters in the north to Heathrow and Uxbridge in the west.

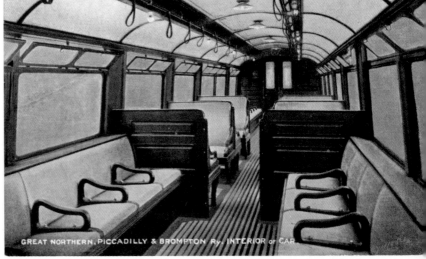

GREAT NORTHERN, PICCADILLY & BROMPTON Ry. INTERIOR of CAR

The view of Piccadilly Circus station (top) reveals the station's colourful tiled decor and the open vestibules of the early rolling stock, while the interior shot shows an extensive use of wood, which would be considered an unacceptable fire risk in the present day.

Notting Hill Gate Station, *c.* 1906

The Central London Railway (Central Line) was the first of London's tubes to connect a suburban area with the city centre. With a flat fare of 2*d*, the 'Tuppeny Tube' initially ran from Shepherds Bush to Bank and from its opening day, 30 July 1900, the service was quicker and cheaper than equivalent ride on the ageing horse buses. The postcard by Messrs. Straker of Notting Hill reveals the station's typical terracotta frontage, which was common to all the line's surface stations. This example succumbed to road widening in the 1950s, after which a new subsurface ticket hall was opened.

The Bank of England and Royal Exchange, *c.* 1909

As a means of boosting passenger numbers, railway companies issued sets of attractive postcards depicting places of interest along their lines. This Celeque card is a little unusual in that a pre-existing card has been overprinted with railway information but the message is conveyed just as effectively. The highlighted station is Bank, then the line's terminus and the only one devoid of surface buildings.

The Arch, Euston Station, *c.* 1905

As the railway age began and gathered strength through the 1830s and 1840s, the first of London's great railway termini began to ring the capital. Euston station was opened by the London & Birmingham Railway Co. in 1837 and was remarkable for the mighty portico (1838) at the station entrance. With what were then the tallest Doric columns in London, the portico was an awesome sight, particularly for those pioneering passengers who were about to experience railway travel for the first time.

London Bridge Station, *c.* 1906

This, London's first terminus, opened with wooden buildings and platforms on 10 October 1836 before a more impressive structure arose from 1840–44. The original operator, the London & Greenwich Railway Co., was soon joined by other railway companies to create the vast and complex station we know today. This classic Oilette postcard captures the bustle of station life from over a century ago.

Victoria Station, c. 1905

A station of two halves resulting from a pair of railway companies, the South Eastern & Chatham with the London, Brighton & South Coast, who opened their adjoining termini in 1860 and 1862 respectively. Their rails crossed the Thames by the first railway bridge, the Grosvenor, to do so. This postcard, sold by the Librarie Continental in Wilton Road, shows the Brighton side of the station as it was before its rebuilding in 1915, while the bulk of the Grosvenor Hotel is seen before a second stage overlooking the station yard arose in 1908. The Chatham side of the station was rebuilt in 1908, and in 1923, both parts of the complex were united as one station. Here, horse buses and cabs compete for space and custom in the station yard where a busy bus station now operates.

The Concourse, Marylebone Station, c. 1906

Opened by the Great Central Railway on 15 March 1899, Marylebone was the last of London's mainline termini and until recent years one of the most underused. The station's rather isolated location had better connections from 27 March 1907 when a Bakerloo tube station opened here – its original name Great Central, was changed to Marylebone on 15 April 1917. Pictured on an Oilette postcard during its early years, Marylebone has since enjoyed a revival in its fortunes and an attractive architectural restoration.

Clapton Station.

Clapton Station, *c.* 1905

Although the Underground network was extending to new areas of London and its suburbs, it did not reach everywhere and in places like Clapton in north-east London there were traditional surface railways to handle commuter and inter-suburban traffic. Clapton station dated from 1872 and was also served by horse trams running between Aldgate and Tottenham.

Horse Trams at Clapton, *c.* 1905

The earliest trams introduced the smoothness of railway travel to the streets alongside the increased effectiveness of the pulling horse on a car running on metal rails rather than the rugged road surfaces of Victorian London. The first tramcars were experimental ones running in 1861 along Bayswater Road and Victoria Street but as their rails stood proud of the road surface, other traffic was obstructed and the experiments failed. The 1870s brought the next generation of trams with rails set into the roadway and from then the horse trams served London well for the remainder of the Victorian era and beyond. This pair of postcards by city publisher Charles Martin convey something of the leisurely pace of life in Edwardian suburban London.

Lea Bridge Road Clapton.

Laying Tracks for Electric Trams, Camberwell Green, 1903
By the turn of the century, horse trams were becoming outmoded and a new generation of tramcars powered by electricity was beginning to transform the system. The electricity was conveyed either by an overhead wire or in a conduit set between the car's running rails. The laying of new tracks and the installation of underground power cables resulted in roadworks on a grand scale but as a large workforce was available, disruption was kept to a minimum. This image from an amateur's album pictures a chaotic scene, but Camberwell's electric trams were up and running within months.

Trams in Hackney Road, Cambridge Heath, *c.* 1905
The new electric cars gave Londoners a taste of luxury street travel, which included a fully enclosed upper deck, a refinement which lay many years in the future for London's buses.

Hackney Road, Cambridge Heath, N. E.

The Kingsway Tram Subway, Kingsway, Holborn, *c.* 1907

While south London could claim the greatest concentration of tram routes, the system's most unusual facility lay to the north of the river – an underground tramway complete with its own stations. This opened on 24 February 1906 and ran beneath what were then London's newest main thoroughfares, Aldwych and Kingsway, with access points at Waterloo Bridge to the south and Kingsway by Southampton Row to the north, with stations at Aldwych and Holborn along the way. Having emerged from the depths via the steep ramp seen here, the cars resumed their usual role as a street tramway. This National series postcard shows the line during the earliest phase of its life when the subway could only take single-deck cars – improvements would soon allow the passage of double-deckers. The first age of the tram in London would end in 1952 and part of the subway would be reborn as the Strand Underpass (1964) – the long disused ramp can still be seen through its railings.

Horse Buses, c. 1906

As time has proved, buses remain the most practical means of street transportation in London. The first of them ran in 1829 on George Shillibeer's pioneering route between Paddington and Bank, the tiny nucleus from which a mighty network evolved through the Victorian era to the present day. Horse power predominated throughout the nineteenth century but there were no route numbers until the final years of horse bus operations and the routes were recognised by the varying colours of the vehicle's liveries. The pair of postcards picture horse buses operated by the London General Omnibus Company, an organisation founded in Paris in 1855 and a direct ancestor of London Transport and today's TfL.

A London Omnibus.

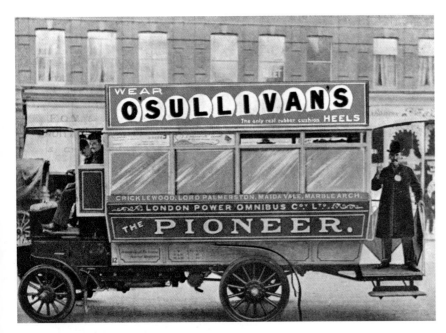

Horse and Motorbuses, Swiss Cottage, Finchley Road

It is 1906 and new motorbuses are replacing their horse-drawn counterparts in increasing numbers. The popularity of the new technology is evident here with a Milnes-Daimler *Vanguard* bus attracting the passengers while the horse buses remain empty. This locally sold postcard also pictures Swiss Cottage, a noted north-west London landmark and a changeover point for buses with fresh horses replacing others at the end of their shift. Having served London well for many decades, the last of the horse buses would run on 4 August 1914 by which time the remaining horses were required for active service in the First World War.

Motorbuses: 'Pioneer' Bus, Cricklewood, *c.* 1904

Although a few experimental steam driven buses had taken to London's streets in the 1800s, the capital had to wait until the early 1900s for the first successful motorbus to appear. Among the first companies to create anything resembling a fleet of viable motorbuses was The London Power Omnibus Co., who with their aptly named 'Pioneer' fleet name operated Scott-Stirling buses from Marble Arch to Kilburn and Cricklewood. Their service began in 1902 with just four of the then in vogue single-deckers with others following, until all were withdrawn and replaced with double-deckers in 1906.

A General Motorbus, Cricklewood, *c.* 1906

The London General Omnibus Co. were busily motorising their fleet in 1906 – this *De Dion* being a typical example of the new breed. There are still no route numbers but the General's red livery would become standard for future London buses and the colour by which they are known worldwide.

A Great Eastern Bus, Great Castle Street, by Great Portland Street, Marylebone, *c.* 1906

As the name implies, The Great Eastern Motor Omnibus Co.'s services connected London's eastern suburbs with the city and West End while other routes extended westwards to Kilburn. The distant corner shop provides a link with the present day with a branch of the still familiar Ryman's the stationers. These postcard images are from monochrome photographs by Ferdinand Kehrhahn, a noted portrayer of the West End.

Lancashire & General Assurance Co.'s Advertising Postcard, *c.* 1925
London's buses have always provided a mobile and highly visible canvas for the advertiser, but here it is an image of a bus itself that has been adapted from an original photograph for some mail shot publicity. The bus company's fleet name has been cheekily 'borrowed' by the advertiser!

A National Bus Conductor, *c.* 1910
As times change, London tends to lose some of the characters that contribute to the life of the city. The most recent departure has been the bus conductor, a victim of the modern generation of driver-only buses, except where a pair of heritage routes still employ old-style Routemaster vehicles. A century earlier, this gentleman had to endure the rigours of open stairs and top deck while collecting fares and preserving order. His vehicle was one of the paraffin-fired steam buses operated by the National Steam Car Co. – these were popular with passengers for their silent running. The card is one of the Celesque series 'London Types'.

London Cabs: Bersey Electric Cabs, Duncannon Street, Strand, c. 1898

The cab trade had also relied on the horse through the 1800s but towards the end of the century an experiment in battery power threatened to end that dominance. Walter Bersey introduced his electric cabs in 1897 and these initially gave good service and were popular, but increasing mechanical problems drove them off the streets by the beginning of the 1900s. Here a quartet of Berseys rank up with hansom cabs against a backdrop of St Martin-in-the-Fields and the National Gallery.

Cab Rank, Holland Park Avenue by Royal Crescent, Kensington, c. 1905

Following its brief flirtation with battery power, the London cab trade returned exclusively to the horse before a new generation of motors began to take over. This scene from a postcard produced for a local stationer shows a typical cab rank complete with examples of the popular two-wheeled cab whose design was patented by Joseph Hansom in 1834. Growlers (four wheelers) are also waiting for the next fare alongside one of the distinctive wooden cabmen's shelters, carefully preserved examples of which can still be seen – this one's gable and bargeboards add a jaunty touch.

The Grand Surrey Canal, Camberwell, *c.* 1906

In the pre-railway age, the need to distribute goods with greater efficiency than was possible on ill surfaced roads became more pressing. A solution came in the form of artificial waterways, canals, a network of which began to connect London with other industrial centres. Much of this was developed to the north of the river with waterways to the Midlands and beyond, but to the south ambitions were more modest. Dating from 1807, the Grand Surrey Canal ran inland from a basin at the Surrey Commercial Docks at Rotherhithe, but despite plans for a navigable waterway running across south London, the canal only reached as far as Peckham. New industry was attracted to canalside locations and here cargoes of timber were brought in from the Thames and there were saw mills along the canal. Salt, whiting and lime works were also set up and, as may be seen, there were rows of canal-side cottages whose residents had an enviable view of life on the waterway. The postcard is by the prolific publisher Card

SURREY CANAL, CAMBERWELL.

House of south London, but despite the vibrancy of the scene it portrays, everything seen here has gone apart from the distant tower of St George's church (1824), which is partly masked by the mast of a sailing barge. Closure of parts of the canal would begin in the 1940s, and by the 1970s it would all be filled in and replaced by the much-needed greenery of Burgess Park. A preserved lime kiln (unseen in the picture), once part of the lime works set up in 1816 by E. R. Burtt, is a sole surviving remnant of this lost industrial landscape.

Local London: the Church of St Mary Abbots, Kensington, c. 1860

Many of London's familiar boroughs originated as rural hamlets and villages, which were caught up in the city's centuries-long expansion into its countryside. In an ongoing process, places that were suburbs a little more than a century ago are now regarded as 'inner city' and real countryside is ever more distant from the centre. Even so, some of the old villages retained something of their former character with preserved buildings amid their newly urbanised surroundings often with individual style to set them apart from their fellows. In the west, opulent Kensington (Chenesitun in the Domesday Book) has undergone a transformation from an unremarkable village in rural Middlesex to a classy residential and cultural area, a home to royalty and from 1901 – a royal borough.

St Mary Abbots' church was a seventeenth rebuilding of an earlier village church, but as new streets of grand Italianate town houses gradually replaced Kensington's old market gardens, Sir Giles Gilbert Scott designed a suitably imposing new church in the Gothic style, complete with the loftiest tower and spire in London – it dates from 1869.

Kensington High Street by Holland Walk, c. 1905

The principal street of old Kensington village developed into one of London's more urbane shopping centres with, from 1868, a new Underground station and from 1870 the first of a trio of fine department stores to rival those of the West End. This Edwardian postcard pictures a more residential High Street from the time when its northern side was made up of four Phillimore Terraces dating from the 1780s. These would be cleared to provide blocks of flats with groundfloor shopping; Troy Court (1931) would replace the houses on the left.

Ladbroke Grove by Lancaster Road, North Kensington, *c.* 1906

Wealth and poverty existed in close proximity in northern Kensington whose main artery, Ladbroke Grove, ran from Holland Park Avenue in the south to a more industrialised landscape in the north with canal-side commercialism, the main line railway out of Paddington, and a malodorous gasworks whose vapours produced a distinctive local atmosphere.

Gentrification has since created a fascinating contrast in modern London with the renowned Notting Hill Carnival, a vibrant and colourful reflection of local West Indian culture.

Portobello Road by Acklam Road, North Kensington, *c.* 1906

Portobello Road straggles across North Kensington on an erratic course that recalls its rural origins as the way to Portobello Farm. This is North Kensington's 'High Street' and is home to a series of markets, including the world-famous antiques market, which has been held at weekends since the 1940s when a few antiques dealers set up here. Before this, horse-trading gypsies were among the first traders in the 1870s and there were costermongers supplying local essentials. This pair of postcards was sold at William Keep's stationery shop in Portobello Road.

44. LONDON — Queens Gate Mansions and Hotel

Charles Volsey, London

Queen's Gate by Manson Mews, South Kensington, c. 1904

With its imposing town houses, hotels and exclusive private schools all leading northwards to Kensington Gardens, this grand boulevard epitomises Victorian South Kensington. Queen's Gate began life in 1855 as Prince Albert Road, the name coming from the Prince Consort who influenced the cultural development of the area – it became Queen's Gate in 1859. The view is at the Brompton end of the street but just misses a sight of the beautiful St Augustine's church (1871), which is off-camera right. The postcard is one of the delicately tinted examples produced in Paris for the publisher Charles Volsey.

Fulham Road by Pelham Crescent, South Kensington, c. 1906

Fulham Road formed a boundary between Kensington and Chelsea while its lengthy course took it further to the one-time village of Fulham. Fulham Road is characterised by an abundance of small shops, which in the early 1900s catered for the residents from the mass of streets that had spread over the old market gardens. Gentrification has since triggered the rise of designer stores and upmarket boutiques. Here, Alice Gooding's stationery shop stands opposite Pelham Crescent and features a crowded window display, including some of the fine coloured postcards that were published for the shop.

Fulham Road

Cheyne Walk from Battersea Bridge, Chelsea, c. 1927

The picturesque Thames-side village of Chelsea with its wharves and dilapidated houses was much loved by artists, including Whister and Turner, but much of the old maritime image was lost from 1874 when the Chelsea Embankment was built on land partly reclaimed from the Thames. On view here is the Embankment wall and to the left is Crosby Hall, a city merchant's mansion, which had been displaced from its original site in Bishopsgate where it had stood since 1475. It had been brought here stone by stone and from 1908–10 re-erected in what was once the garden of Sir Thomas More's Chelsea home. To the right is the seventeenth-century tower of All Saints, Chelsea Old church, which would suffer wartime destruction but rise again in the 1950s. Parts of the church still show masonry from the fourteenth and subsequent centuries.

Cheyne Walk, Chelsea, c. 1904

These remnants of old Chelsea were once separated from the Thames by the narrowest of roads before the Embankment divorced them from the river. Victorian flats (1886) rise in the distance and in later years more flats would replace these quaint cottages with their bootmaker's shop.

King's Road, Chelsea

Long a haunt of the artistic and fashionable, King's Road began life as a private street used by King Charles II when travelling between London and Hampton Court Palace. When the public were finally allowed to use the road in 1830, King's Road soon developed as Chelsea's principal shopping street, but as artists and writers also found the area to their taste, there was always an element of the quirky and offbeat to the street and its shops. In the 'Swinging Sixties', King's Road blossomed into a boutique-lined parade of fashionable emporia and a place where young trendies gathered to flaunt the latest styles in clothing. This pair of postcards show King's Road in Edwardian times when, in the upper view, Chelsea Town Hall (1886) is about to be remodelled and, on the left, Chelsea Palace (1903–57) is a flourishing theatre where the likes of George Robey and Harry Lauder entertained. The lower view looks westwards from Walpole Street whose corner was then graced by William Battersby's jewellery and pawnbroking shop, a reminder that hardship still existed amid Chelsea's affluence.

SLOANE AVENUE
MANSIONS

SLOANE AVENUE
CHELSEA — S·W

Telephone :
KENSINGTON **7020.**

Telegrams & Cables :
CONPROPS, LONDON

300 ROOMS

AND DINING ROOM, Etc·

Furnished One-Room Flats with
Kitchenette and Bathroom, including Service from **£3 3s. 0d.**
per week,

Furnished Two-Room Flats with
Kitchenette and Bathroom, including Service from **£4 4s. 0d.**
per week,

Sloane Avenue Mansions, Sloane Avenue, Chelsea, Mid-1930s

A poor area of small streets between Fulham and Kings Roads was revitalised in the 1920s by the cutting through of a new street, Sloane Avenue. By the 1930s, this had become colonised by smart new town houses and blocks of luxury flats, of which Sloane Avenue Mansions was a fine example. The rental prices outlined on this promotional postcard may look tempting today but in the 1930s these were considered expensive.

Elizabeth Street by Gerald Road, South Belgravia, c. 1906

This is one of the mixed residential and shopping streets running southwards towards Victoria station and Pimlico. Dressmakers occupied many of the premises in Edwardian times alongside the usual domestic stores, but the wealth of Belgravia has always influenced life here and a profusion of smart exclusive shops in the present day perpetuates that image. The postcard is by Charles Martin of Aldermanbury and is one of the few tinted versions in an output of over 3,000 monochrome view cards.

Battersea Square, Battersea, *c.* 1906

London's old Thames-side villages tantalise with their handfuls of aged buildings hinting at a long lost rural and maritime lifestyle. At Battersea the surrounding fields and market gardens made way in the nineteenth century for mass housing and industry, but the old village centre retained enough of its former self to recall more leisured times. Emerging from post-war gloom, Battersea became trendy and an overflow for those priced out of Chelsea, with the worst of its outdated housing stock replaced by modern estates and the remaining terraced houses perked up by gentrification. Battersea Square is at the heart of old Battersea and it is seen here in a postcard by Card House when, in Edwardian days, it was filled with domestic stores and housed, on the right, Battersea Square Post Office. There is a distant glimpse of Battersea Church Road leading to the river where there were Thames-side wharves – ships still moored in the shadow St Mary's, the old village church.

Battersea Square, *c.* 1912

A postcard by R. J. Johns pictures more of old Battersea village.

Turret Grove, Off North Street, Clapham, *c.* 1912

With its hilltop location, leafy common and historic Old Town it is easy to imagine Clapham in its earlier guise as a country retreat for well-to-do Londoners and a place to which they could escape the plague and fire ravaged city in 1665 and 1666 respectively. Housebuilding in the nineteenth century joined Clapham to London's expanding built-up area but there were many attractive streets like Turret Grove, which continue to show a mixture of typical south London housing styles.

Clapham High Street Looking Towards Clapham Road, *c.* 1912

Ribbon development beside this major highway linking Surrey with London and expansion of old Clapham village contributed to the appearance of the street, which here shows many of the characteristics of a maturing London suburb early in the 1900s. These typically include the shops on the left, which were put up in the front gardens of older houses to catch the passing trade. The street was served by electric trams and there was a new cinema, which had opened in 1910 as The Electric Pavilion – it would remain in business as The Pavilion until 1957. This is a further pair of postcards by the prolific R. J. Johns who specialised in the photography of side streets whose residents could post the cards showing 'our street'.

Atlantic Road, Brixton, c. 1905

In the eighteenth century, Brixton was a village in rural Surrey, but in the nineteenth century, its proximity to London and the arrival of a network of railway lines increased its appeal as a place for Londoners to live and turned it into a typical Victorian suburb. The 1950s and 1960s brought immigration and the unique energy generated by the arrival of a new population from the West Indies. Behind the camera and beneath the overhead rail lines, Atlantic Road's boisterous street markets would undergo a transition from Cockney to Caribbean style in the decades to come.

Brixton Road, c. 1906

With three department stores, theatres, cinemas and busy markets, Brixton soon established itself as one of the livelier shopping and entertainments districts of south London. This Cameragraph postcard pictures two of Brixton's major stores, Bon Marche, centre, and Quin & Axten's, right, who were holding a summer sale. The railway bridge boldly proclaims the local newspaper, *The Brixtonian*, which cost one penny.

Coldharbour Lane, Loughborough Junction, Brixton, *c.* 1906

A suburb of the mid-Victorian era set around a complex of railway viaducts and bridges, all completed by 1872. Here, the Warrior, a fine Victorian pub, stands at the corner of Belinda Road, while David Greig's shop a few doors away recalls a famous grocery chain that began locally in Atlantic Road in 1888.

Acre Lane, Brixton, *c.* 1906

The urbanisation of Brixton in the nineteenth century cost these eighteenth-century houses their front gardens, but there were new neighbourhood shops to compensate for the lost greenery and cater to the growing population. This postcard was produced for Mrs Emily James' confectionery shop where the windows are filled with a fine selection of local and other view cards. Mrs James' shop is flanked by Ernest Gingell's Dining Rooms, left, which dispensed 'cuts from the joint', bloaters and kippers, while to the right a display of intoxicants fills the windows of wine and spirit merchant William Sewell.

The Elephant & Castle, Southwark, *c.* 1906

'The Elephant' is one of those areas of London whose name is derived from a single building, and in this instance it is an eighteenth-century coaching inn on the road to Kent. In the nineteenth century, rebuilding turned the plain old Elephant & Castle into a flamboyant Victorian monster, but in post-war years, with the area in ruins, an emasculated Elephant would be reborn amid the enormous roundabouts that would try to tame one of the most complex traffic junctions in south London. This pair of locally published postcards captures something of the chaos of Edwardian days when electric trams on a multitude of routes fought their way through equine traffic jams of epic proportions.

**Wooden Houses, Collingwood Street (Now Colombo Street),
Off Blackfriars Road, Southwark, c. 1905**

Wooden houses were once commonplace in London, but in the years following the Great Fire brick construction was preferred. Wood was, however, still used for lowlier dwellings like these examples from the 1700s. They were put up in a lane then called The Green Walk in a semi-rural area noted for its 'tenter grounds' – open fields where cloth was stretched and dried in the open air. By the 1900s, wooden houses in inner London were rare indeed, but these ones lasted longer than most and were finally demolished in 1948 having suffered war damage. The adjoining St Mark's church (through the railings, right) was also damaged but rose again in 1959.

Old Kent Road and Bricklayer's Arms, Bermondsey, c. 1906

The modern version of the old Roman road from London to Dover traversed a lively slice of traditional south-east London with the Bricklayer's Arms one of its more noted hostelries. The Bricklayer's Arms gave its name to an early railway station (1844) – this would end its days as a parcel depot. The postcard by F. Henschel & Co. of Old Kent Road pictures an Elephant-bound tram and crowded pavements by a busy shopping parade, all of which would fall victim to the massive Bricklayer's Arms flyover scheme in the 1960s.

Southwark Park Road by Blue Anchor Lane, Bermondsey, *c.* 1906
Southwark Park Road takes a lengthy and tortuous course between Rotherhithe and Bermondsey, its populous neighbourhood providing ample custom for the street's variety of shops and market stalls – the latter continues to include the popular 'Blue Market'. Old-style horse trams once negotiated the throngs of shoppers, but after the last horse-drawn car ran in Rotherhithe in 1915, tramway operation ceased and electrification was not proceeded with. Another of F. Henschel's local views shows the prominent Blue Anchor pub standing by Blue Anchor Lane, which once wound its way through a lost landscape of meadows and market gardens. The pub is an 1875 rebuilding of a picturesque weather-boarded inn whose hospitality once refreshed a rustic clientele.

Evelyn Street, Deptford, *c.* 1904
Rich in naval history, the one-time fishing village of Deptford lies beside the Thames between Rotherhithe and Greenwich. Evelyn Street is an ancient highway linking the two, its name coming from diarist John Evelyn (1620–1706) who lived close to the Royal Naval Dockyard. The postcard is by one of the more respected photographers of south-east London, Perkins & Son of Lewisham. Their study of Evelyn Street shows some of the lengthy terraces of plain-fronted houses from the late 1700s and early 1800s along with the Telegraph pub, right, and the premises of farrier, ship's chandler and general smith William Parr at the far right.

Corbetts Lane, Rotherhithe New Road, *c.* 1910

With its lengthy frontage to the river, Rotherhithe grew through the maritime trade, with the first of the facilities that preceded Surrey Commercial Docks arriving in 1697. Housing for dockers and other local industries spread across the old Thames floodplain with quality sometimes sacrificed for quantity. The twentieth century brought war damage and the clearance of much of the old housing to make way for a new landscape of sprawling housing estates. This modest terrace is pictured on an amateur photographer's postcard, with the cottages overlooking a 'rope-walk', a long strip of land used by rope-makers. A distant fragment of roofline can be seen from the Jolly Gardeners pub in Rotherhithe New Road, the only building to survive here.

Reculver Road by Alpine Road, Rotherhithe, *c.* 1910

A glimpse into a lost neighbourhood of old Rotherhithe where its younger element is out in force. The London County Council's Silwood Estate would transform this area from 1955 followed by a further rebuilding for the twenty-first century.

Narrow Street from Medland Street and Broad Street (The Highway), Ratcliff, c. 1918

Life in Ratcliff, on the Middlesex shore of the Thames, downstream from Wapping, was bound up with seafaring and ship repairing with the early 1900s seeing ship's chandlers, and mast and sail makers still working amid a profusion of wharfingers. As seen in this amateur's snapshot, Narrow Street runs down to the river at Ratcliff Cross Stairs before turning left and following the Thames to the old lime-burning area of Limehouse where Oriental seamen and their families created London's first Chinatown from the 1890s. Also seen are the Phoenix Biscuit Works where ship's biscuit was made. The streets immense character would prove popular in modern times with luxurious warehouse conversions and upmarket apartments.

Cable Street, St George-in-the-East, c. 1906

Running from Royal Mint Street to Limehouse, Cable Street bisects a colourful section of the old maritime East End, its name probably originating in the eighteenth century from the rope- and cable-makers who worked here. This was also one of London's Jewish quarters, and in pre-war years there was a variety of small shops serving that community. The view shows St George's town hall (1860) – St George-in-the-East is one of the Tower Hamlets, now part of the modern London Borough of Tower Hamlets. The emphasis today is on the modern housing estates, which arose from post-war dereliction.

Watney Street by Chapman Street, Shadwell, *c.* 1906

Picture postcards first appeared in Britain in 1894 but it was from 1901 that the demand for local neighbourhood views gathered strength, and by 1906 almost everywhere in this country had been pictured on a card. In some areas of London the coverage was intensive with almost every street having its own postcards, while in others, like the inner East End, few postcards ever appeared. Nevertheless, stationer and tobacconist Charles Fielding was on hand to supply the area's Cockney and Jewish population with his colourful range of new-style local views, which were specially produced for his shop – this naturally enough featured on one of the cards, as seen here.

Watney Market, Watney Street, Commercial Road, Shadwell, *c.* 1906

Continuing this sequence of Fielding views is an image of Watney Street, a classic East End street of small domestic stores, many of which occupied by shopkeepers who had traded here through several decades. As ever, the market barrows brought in the crowds, and even when parts of the street were in ruins after the Blitz trading continued. A rebuilt market would open in the 1970s. Commercial Road can be seen in the distance – it was laid out early in the nineteenth century as a road route between the City of London and the newly opened East and West India Docks.

Ratcliff Highway/St George Street (Now The Highway), St George-in-the-East, c. 1906.

The murder of seven people here in 1811 enhanced the street's existing notoriety as a centre of vice; in the hope of new respectability, the street name was changed to St George Street. As seen here, most of the shops were run by Jewish immigrant traders, including Libman's, left, while the Jolly Sailor pub next door was a reminder that the river was close at hand. Further along was a noteworthy emporium owned by Albert Jamrach, a naturalist and wild animals dealer whose stock sometimes included exotic creatures brought home by local seamen.

Eighteenth-Century Cottages, Pennington Street by John's Hill, c. 1906

When first built, these tiny houses enjoyed a semi-rural location but a century later the building of the extensive London Dock complex transformed life in the neighbourhood and left the cottages in the shadow of the mighty walls which enclosed the docks. The cottages would linger on through the 1930s, but increasing dereliction and the Blitz would finally end their lengthy lives.

St. James the Great Bethnal Green Road.

Bethnal Green Road by Pollard Row, Bethnal Green, *c.* 1907

This sequence of local neighbourhood views continues with a pair of images picturing two more of the bustling street markets of the old East End. Bethnal Green was once a pleasant village in rural Middlesex but it became increasingly urbanised as silk-weavers from Spitalfields moved in and labyrinthine complexes of streets began to replace the old agricultural land. Bethnal Green Road was given a new look from around 1879 – it is seen here running eastwards towards the former village green and passing St James the Great (1844), which was known locally as The Red Church from the colour of its brickwork.

Chrisp Street, Poplar, *c.* 1905

Even for a populous area like Poplar, this is a spectacular turnout of locals, all anxious that their face should appear on a new postcard by publisher Stengel & Co. The street itself ran for half a mile and was crammed with shops, barrows and stalls – it was a famous hunting ground for Edwardian East Enders who loved their markets and a bargain. War would wreck the street, but a new market would arise in 1951 alongside a housing estate built as an architectural showpiece for the Festival of Britain.

Chrisp Street, looking South, Poplar.

Nile Street From East Road.

Nile Street, Hoxton (Shoreditch), *c.* 1906

Hoxton and Shoreditch grew up as part of rural Middlesex, but ribbon development along their principal highways brought a more urban environment as London expanded. By the seventeenth century the area saw new housing and industry, which by Victorian timess had eroded the remaining greenery and there was overcrowding and poverty.

There were typical inner-city neighbourhoods by Edwardian times, some of which were pictured by bookseller and stationer Albert Knowland for the new medium of postal view cards. These were sold in Knowland's shop (left and page 4), while his neighbour Charles Offord's eel pie shop served cockney favourites, including pie and mash for 2*d* and pea soup for 1*d*. There was also a fine Victorian pub, the Duke of Wellington, and an assortment of market barrows.

Citizen Dwellings, Nile Street, Hoxton (Shoreditch), *c.* 1906

Parts of London were notorious for their slum housing conditions, but from the 1860s the charitable work of the Peabody and Guinness Trusts began to build blocks of model dwellings for impoverished workers. Shoreditch was the first Metropolitan Borough of London to provide similar accommodation – these blocks in Nile Street arose in 1896 and, in a city that was still mostly gaslit, had electric lighting from the outset.

Citizen Dwellings.

Dawsons Corner, City Road.

Dawson Bros, Linen Drapers and Furnishers, City Road, and East Road, Shoreditch, *c.* **1906**

Generations of housewives flocked to this popular emporium, which enjoyed lengthy frontages to two major roads. City Road, left, was in the 1750s part of the New Road, London's first northern bypass – it later divided the old Metropolitan Boroughs of Finsbury and Shoreditch. Further along (off-camera left) was the location of the Eagle Tavern, of 'Pop Goes the Weasel' fame.

Chapel Market, Angel, Islington, *c.* **1905**

This traditional cockney street market served a populous slice of inner North London, the stalls and barrows supplementing the shops that lined the road. Among them and seen here with a striped sunblind was a branch of John Sainsbury, provisions merchant, seen in the days before the firm evolved into the mighty retailing giant we know today. The market remains vibrant in the present day, but a little of its old-time atmosphere lingers on.

Chapel Street, Islington, London.

King's Cross, St Pancras, *c.* 1907

Through their ability to capture the flavour of an area with a few well-chosen images, multiple view postcards have always had popular appeal. This one in the Chaucer series is part of a lengthy set and highlights a busy quarter of London famous for its great transport interchanges and nightmarish road traffic.

In common with many districts of London, King's Cross originated as a village – this one was Battlebridge, at a crossing of the River Fleet. The laying out in 1756 of the New Road, here called Euston Road, brought an influx of traffic, and when in 1830 a statue of King George IV was put up, the area was styled 'The King's Crossroads'.

Top left: King's Cross station (Great Northern Railway) was built on the site of a smallpox hospital and opened in 1852. Here it is fronted by the then new Great Northern, Piccadilly & Brompton Railway's tube station, which opened on 15 December 1906.

Top right: Euston Theatre of Varieties, Euston Road. Built in 1900, the Euston had a varied career under an assortment of names, and in its heyday it attracted many popular acts, including the legendary Harry Lauder. The building also operated as a cinema until the all-conquering Bingo saw out the theatre's last days in 1969.

Bottom right: St Pancras old church, Pancras Road. The discovery of a seventh-century altar here highlighted the antiquity of one of London's earliest church sites, and there are surviving fragments from the twelfth and thirteenth centuries among the rebuildings of later years.

Bottom centre: St Pancras new church, Upper Woburn Place, is a much admired neo-Grecian church (1822), built to serve congregations from the houses then being built around the New Road, part of the northern expansion of Bloomsbury.

Bottom left: St Pancras town hall, Pancras Road. The vestry hall, later St Pancras town hall, dated from 1875, but was replaced by a new facility in Euston Road in 1937. The old Metropolitan Borough of St Pancras has been part of the London Borough of Camden since 1965.

EGENTS PARK ROAD, N.W.

Regent's Park Road, Primrose Hill, *c.* 1908

Primrose Hill is a noted viewpoint to the north of Regent's Park and the location of a smart residential area that grew up in the mid-1800s. Shopping parades in Princess and Regent's Park Roads supplied local requisites and there was E. W. Wood's fancy goods warehouse with its colourful postcards of local views.

Oppidans Mews, Primrose Hill, *c.* 1908

Mews streets are usually found in the well-to-do residential areas of central London – suburban ones are less common. These old stables housed horses, grooms, stable hands and carriages, but as the age of the motor car took hold many old mews became the province of the limousine and chauffeur. Later gentrification saw these cobbled byways blossom into picturesque residential enclaves – in this example, rampant Virginia creeper threatens to engulf the street. Another postcard from E. W. Wood.

OPPIDAN'S MEWS, PRIMROSE HILL, N.W.

Nugent Terrace, St John's Wood, c. 1907

St John's Wood was part of the former Metropolitan Borough of St Marylebone – it developed from the 1820s, partly in place of the ill-favoured settlement of Portland Town. The area is characterised by leafy streets of pretty classical and Gothic houses, some of which have succumbed to luxury flat-building in the twentieth century. St John's Wood boasts an elegant High Street filled with smart shops, supplemented by local shopping streets like Nugent Terrace, all of which contribute to the area's popular village-like environment.

Boundary Road, St John's Wood, c. 1907

The boundary marked by the street name was that between the Metropolitan Boroughs of St Marylebone and Hampstead, now the City of Westminster and the London Borough of Camden. This postcard was published by stationer E. W. White and was sold at his shop, which doubled as a post office, a common arrangement in former times – there were two such facilities in Boundary Road. E. W. White's shop is seen here, its window displays having attracted some attention.

Queen Victoria in Edgware Road, June 1897

Edgware Road has not found fame as a royal processional route, yet in June 1897 the then rather drab street was treated to a fine display of pageantry. The Royal Train from Windsor had brought Queen Victoria to Paddington station, from where the Queen was driven to Buckingham Palace, accompanied by a colourful military escort. The occasion was Her Majesty's Diamond Jubilee, which was further celebrated by the erection of a ceremonial arch across Edgware Road (far left).

The highway itself dates from Roman times as Watling Street and has long served as a route from Marble Arch (formerly Tyburn) to London's north-western suburbs.

Westbourne Grove, Bayswater (Paddington), c. 1906

This remained a rural way until the 1840s, when London's expansion brought new housing to this part of Paddington alongside a lengthy shopping centre. This went on to feature a variety of department stores, including the early ventures of the entrepreneurial William Whiteley, 'the universal provider', one of which is seen on this postcard by J. Beagles & Co. Whiteley's shops were united in 1911 in a vast and palatial emporium in Queen's Road (Queensway).

Dudding Hill, Neasden, opposite Gladstone Park. £10 down and 10s. 7d. per week for 15 years will purchase one of these houses. Lease 999 years. Ground Rent £8.0.0. No law costs: no road-making charges. Within 2 minutes Neasden Station, Metn. Electric. Baker St.; Season Ticket £1.2.6 per quarter. Excellent through service to City. Apply—Jno. C. Hill & Co., Office on Estate, 2, Burnley Rd., Dudding Hill Lane, Neasden, or 14, Archway Roa', N. 'Phone 2404 N.   1, Adelaide St., W.C.
Photo. CLARK & MANN.

Housebuilder's Promotional Postcard: New Housing in Dudding Hill, Willesden, c. 1908

London's growth continued apace through the Edwardian decade, with the popular bay-windowed terraces of Victorian times maintaining their appeal. These new ones in Willesden were larger than most, but the prices publicised here may seem wonderfully cheap – yet of course they were no more affordable than in the present day. These houses preceded the phenomenon of 'Metroland', the great interwar housing schemes promoted by the Metropolitan Railway alongside their lines through Middlesex and beyond.

Kilburn Park Road, Shewing   St. Augustines Church

St Augustine, Kilburn Park Road from Carlton Vale, c. 1906

Grand and inspiring church buildings can be found throughout London. Here, J. L. Pearson's mighty edifice rises high above the lowlier buildings around it. The church was built from 1870 to 1877, but it took until 1898 to complete the 254-foot spire. The church and its neighbourhood are located close to the former Metropolitan Boroughs of Paddington and Willesden, now the City of Westminster and the London Borough of Brent.

Tramcars' Afterlife: Poplar Square School, Poplar Place, Bayswater, Paddington,

Victorian horse-drawn tramcars were withdrawn from London's streets during the Edwardian era, as modern electric cars took their place. Much of the old stock was scrapped, but some old horse cars found new roles to extend their lives. New uses included conversion to static holiday homes, garden sheds or roadside refreshment outlets, for which their shape was ideal. This photograph reveals an unusual, possibly unique, use for redundant horse tramcars – classrooms for Poplar Square Infants' School, which opened late in 1912.

The locality was the hinterland behind Bayswater Road, Queens Road (Queensway), Moscow Road and Caroline Place – well-to-do in the present day, but a century ago beset by poverty, with rag merchants and chimney sweeps among those scraping a living here. Poplar Place was originally home to Bayswater Ragged School, which opened in 1850 and gave a basic education to the most deprived children.

Poplar Square offered a healthy outdoor educational experience with lessons taken on a tram's top deck or at desks brought out into the playground. This was a large grassy area with a sandpit, which was popular at playtime.

The photograph records a day within a fortnight of the school's opening, but it appears to have had a short life, for all traces of it vanished long ago.